WITHOUT AN ALLY

The Secret Lives of LGBTQ+ People During World War II

Morgan Sandner Beatty

ACKNOWLEDGEMENTS

To my wife, without your support this would still be a file on my Google Drive. And a special thank you to Gregory, who gave me the idea, and Jordan, a great beta reader.

TABLE OF CONTENTS

INTRODUCTION

In the spring of 2022, a couple of months into my first job out of college, I was continuing to cut my teeth in customer service in hopes of working my way up the ranks in the museum. It was that spring that my best friend from college called me up to tell me about the "Gay Day " his school had just held to celebrate Pride month, as they are not in school during June. He was in his final months of student teaching history in the city we had graduated from in North Carolina. He was calling to give me back that spark of purpose because by the first class bell that day all of the Pride decorations in the hall had been ripped down by students. Both of us had gotten most, if not all, of our education in North Carolina and neither of us had learned any LGBTQ+ history until college. This is when one of our wonderful professors taught a class on Biological Human

Variation and taught us about intersex people. She would later get me involved with the NAMES Project when they brought multiple panels from the AIDS quilt to our city leading me to receive the Julia Boseman Award from my University for recognition of leadership and contributions in educational, social, and/or political activism for the LGBTQ+ community when I graduated in May of 2021.

We both thought this would be a great time to integrate some history into his lesson plans that we had been deprived of in our education. I had planned to come back to our city for unrelated reasons at the beginning of May, which is when he would be in a unit about World War II, so it began. We had planned to ask if I could be a guest lecturer about LGBTQ+ issues in World War II, we brainstormed what we should talk about and eventually narrowed our scope to be able to fit it into a 45-minute lecture. We would talk about the big three on each side, the United Kingdom, the United States, and the

Soviet Union for the Allied Powers and Japan, Italy, and Germany for the Axis Powers.

Unfortunately, the lesson plan was denied, and it sat untouched in my Google Drive for about a year before I decided to do something with it. The research was done, it just needed to be reformatted and expanded upon as there was no time constraint limiting my research.

When I rediscovered the skeleton of research, I intended only to give the background of the legality of being an LGBTQ+ individual in the big three of the Allied and Axis powers before the Second World War as well as accounts from people who were wronged by these regulations. Of course, there were more countries involved including France which was part of the Allied powers until they were invaded by Nazi Germany beginning on May 10th, 1940 which made for an interesting divide as the Soviet Union and the United States would not join the Allied powers until 1941, after France had fallen.

Another force to join the Allied powers in 1941 was China, eager to oppose Japan as they continued to do during the Second Sino-Japanese War (July 7th, 1937- September 9th, 1945) allowing American bombers to use their air bases for a shorter range to their Japanese targets. It was not until I started research for a second topic that stemmed from this one that I found myself disappointed that I was not adding research on France in either project as my research in my second project led to me realizing I misunderstood the timeline of events. So then I decided to expand my research to include France as well as China which gave me great pleasure when I discovered the personal narratives I got to expand upon.

Including LGBTQ+ narratives in historical analysis allows us to explore the struggles, achievements, and contributions of queer individuals throughout different time periods and cultures. It helps us understand the impact of societal attitudes and discrimination on LGBTQ+

lives, as well as the ways in which queer individuals have navigated and resisted those challenges. Despite scouring information regarding Italy, I could not find an account longer than that of Giuseppe B. to add as a first-hand account of what it was like during or just after World War II for an LGBTQ+ person in Italy, therefore, unfortunately, that section is cut shorter than its counterparts.

More often than not lesbianism is not considered, it is brought up in Nazi Germany as a consideration to ban however it is not passed. Though the "oath clause" in the United Kingdom specified male homosexuality as opposed to homosexuality in general, the ambiguity of the term "gross indecency" was utilized against female military members to discharge them and strip them of any metals during World War II despite no written law being against female homosexuality. In the United States psychiatric screening for homosexuality during military induction beginning in 1944 for the Women's

Army Corps resulted in "Blue Discharges", a dishonorable discharge for those found "unfit for service".

Unfortunately, bisexuality is difficult to pinpoint in historical documentation unless the person self-identifies, and as it was only coined in 1866 in the book *Psychopathia Sexualis* by psychologist Richard Von Krafft-Ebing many people may have been unaware of this area between heterosexuality and homosexuality. Due to this we have the rare opportunity to learn about Anne Frank's story, while not explicitly identified as LGBTQ+ in her diary, hints at the complexities of identity and personal exploration. Her musings about curiosity, desire, and affection toward girls shed light on the inner world of a young girl grappling with her own identity.

In regards to representation of gender across the LGBTQ+ acronym throughout this book, in some instances, such as the Soviet Union we see personal growth including implementing gender-affirming healthcare for 36

intersex individuals before the hard work of a
revolution was broken down by the Stalin era
and it is difficult to find first-hand accounts about
these individuals.

AXIS POWERS

CHAPTER ONE

JAPAN

Shintoism, an ancient religion of Japan dating back to 1000 BC, centers on the belief in numerous deities. The first two gods to arise from this were Kunitokotachi and Amenominakanushi who were dual-gendered/genderless. Shinto, meaning "the way the gods", believe all people are fundamentally good, and since sex, regardless of the biological sex of your partner, was an expression of love it was an inherently benign act. This religion would be most prominent until 1945, as westernization and other factors such as population numbers took a toll on the view the Japanese masses had on what would later be known as "LGBTQ" issues.

During the Tokugawa (or Edo) period, the historical practices identified by scholars as homosexual include *nanshoku* (男色), *shudō* (衆道), and *wakashudō* (若衆道). The term *nanshoku* (男色) directly translates to "male colors" however the character 色 ('color') has the added meaning of "lust" and was widely used to refer to male-to-male sex in the pre-modern era of Japan. The term *shudō* (衆道) is abbreviated from *wakashudō* (若衆道) which translates to "the way of adolescent boys". The Wakashū (younger men) could be compared to a third gender, they wore distinct kimonos with hairstyles featuring a shaved crown and long forelocks which were exclusive to them. Their beauty was noted to be distinct from women or mature men and they were commonly compared to cherry blossoms. Once the Wakashū came of age, they transitioned to more masculine fashion and grooming and it was presumed that they would marry women and bear children. That being said, as the Meiji Restoration began in 1868 anti-homosexual laws would be passed such as making sodomy illegal from 1872 however this was repealed in 1882.

Between the substantial population loss caused by the Second Sino-Japanese War from July 7th, 1937 to September 9th, 1945 and the Second World War officially joined with the signing of the Tripartite pact with Germany and Italy on September 27th, 1940 in conjunction with the ideals pushed by westernization homosexual relations were seen as something that hindered their population.

During World War II, Japan occupied various countries starting in December of 1941, with Guam, Wake Island, and Hong Kong followed by the Philippines, the Dutch East Indies (Indonesia), Malaya, Singapore, and Burma in 1942. Military correspondence within the Imperial Japanese Army reveals that the aim for facilitating comfort stations was essentially to reduce or prevent rape crimes by Japanese army personnel, to reduce venereal diseases among

Japanese troops, and to prevent leakage of military secrets by civilians who were in contact with Japanese officers. Japanese troops forced hundreds of thousands of women from Korea, the Philippines, Vietnam, China, and other countries they were occupying into brothels. For several years he and his companions, other "comfort gays", were put to forced labor and abused sexually by Japanese soldiers, as the *ianfu* (慰安婦) or "comfort women" were abused. In this section we read about the life of Walter Dempster Jr., a gay cross-dressing nightclub performer turned comfort gay.

Walter Dempster Jr.

Walter Dempster Jr. was born May 20th, 1924 in the Philippine Islands, his father had passed away in 1933 and his mother remarried an American man giving Dempster two step-sisters. By 1939 he had grown his hair long and started dressing his sisters' clothing, much to the displeasure of his mother and especially his brother who would physically abuse him for this.

He joined a group of six cross-dressing performers. He got his stage name, Walterina Markova from Alicia Markova, the Russian ballerina. She came to the Philippines to perform and his friends told him that they would borrow Markova's name from her and give it to him. Dempster would perform regularly in Pasay at Lonapor, Subic Bay, and Angeles Nightclub, the latter of which he would regularly perform for the United States Navy who were none the wiser about Dempster being male due to his feminine costume complete with a rubber bust. He remembers that the owner of the club would gather his employees to debrief them saying: "Tonight our special dancer is a gay, but please don't tell the customers."

The Japanese arrived in the Philippines in January of 1942, then officials came to their door asking if they had an American living with them and they surrendered his step-father. Officials wandered the streets and were less than tolerant of Dempster's lack of respect for them. This caused an official to bring him to the barber shop, cutting his long hair. Returning home in tears he was met by his mother who told him that's what he got for being gay. Fortunately, he was able to borrow a wig from a friend of his so he could continue to masquerade as a woman at night.

During the occupation, he stopped dancing in Pasay and began performing at the Tsubaki Nightclub in Manila for Japanese patrons where he made friends with various performers including one who had moved there to avenge his family that was killed by the Japanese in their province in Cebu.

This club was relatively new and had slow days on occasion, one night, in particular, the performer from Cebu convinced Dempster and another performer from the club to take a walk in their evening gowns and happened upon a group of Japanese officials, they invited

Dempster and back to their hotel and as the evening began to heat up Dempster had been made, the official he had been sharing the night with had placed his hand on his groin and began screaming "Bakero! You are not a real woman, you're a boy!" and instructed the other officials to check their girls. They were then taken to Japanese military police at the Rizal Memorial Baseball Stadium where the officials were ordered to punish them for their deception they were sodomized at bayonet point and then ordered to clean. This abuse would continue throughout the two weeks spent at the stadium until they were taken next door to the Japanese headquarters and barracks to be relocated to other places outfitted to be barracks such as the Harrison Plaza where the cycle of abuse continued.

One day three of them were woken up in the middle of the night and put on a truck, They suspected the officials planned to kill them, and to their luck, the truck stalled in Esda, an area of primarily rice fields, and as it was so late they were able to run and not get caught due to the cloak of night. After running for about half an hour Dempster found himself at home not being able to recognize himself in a mirror, his hair turned to an afro, his long gown torn to a mini skirt. The three of them fled to Batangas to continue working in various cabarets together.

The performer from Cebu went on to exact his revenge, picking up Japanese officials as a prostitute, bringing them to the Walled City, and proceeding to murder them with a dagger sheathed under his dress and steal their money. The noises were thought to be heard by officials in the other room with no question. He would murder five officials before being wanted.

Once captured he was brought to San Beda College which was made into the headquarters occupied by the Japanese at the time. They tied him up to a big stake at the main gate and kept him in the sun for almost two weeks, where he was tortured by the officials putting out their cigarettes on his skin.

After American soldiers returned, his stepfather attempted to bring Dempster and his two stepsisters to America with him however Dempster changed his mind in the truck on the way there.

In 1995, Dempster's manager, Councilor Justo Justo, whom he was employed by to do makeup for his performers, asked for an interesting story and Dempster told him of his time as a comfort gay. Three years later, Justo presented the story to director Gil Portes, another year passed before Director Portes and his crew came to Justo's office to interview Dempster. During filming Dempster stayed on set to give pointers to the actors. They filmed in locations such as the Army Navy Club where he used to perform. *Markova: Comfort Gay* was released in 2000 and won the Best Actor and Best Actress Awards, as well as Best International Picture.

He spent the last years of his life at the Home for the Golden Gays, an assisted living home founded in 1975 for elderly LGBTQ people in Pasay, Philipines. He passed away at the age of 81 due to injuries caused by being struck by a bicyclist in 2005.

Aston, William George. "Chronicles of Japan from the Earliest Times to A.D. 697." Story. In The Nihongi:

Chronicles of Japan from the Earliest Times to A.D. 697. s.n., 1990.

Klein, Ronald D. "Markova: Wartime Comfort Gay in the Philippines." Intersections: Gender, History, and Culture in the Asian Context no. 13, August 2006.

Reichert, Jim. In The Company of Men: Representations of Male-Male Sexuality in Meiji Literature. Stanford,

CA: Stanford University Press, 2006.

Underwood, A. C. Shintoism: The Indigenous Religion of Japan. United States: Pomona Press, 2013.

CHAPTER TWO

ITALY

In 1930, Benito Mussolini implemented the Italian Penal Code, also known as the Rocco Code of Criminal Law, which notably did not address homosexuality. However, by 1932, arguments emerged suggesting that the inclusion of such laws would publicize homosexuality. Italian stereotypes say that Italians were naturally manly therefore homosexuality was scarce. Fascist officials in conjunction with their Nazi counterparts saw homosexuality as a threat, classed with abortion and birth control as a threat to the health of the Italian race, though Mussolini never commented on this, evidence suggests he knew of the persecution and approved.

The oppression of homosexuals was consistent throughout the mid-1930s with a spike during WW2. They would be sent into "internal exile" (*confino*) on the island of San Domino in the Tremiti chain in the Adriatic Sea and the island of Ustica in the Tyrrhenian Sea where they would commonly pass away due to poor diet or health complications onset from the environment of the island. According to police records, 88 political prisoners and 298 common criminals were exiled after being found guilty of homosexuality or other terms that were used interchangeably with homosexuality such as; pederasty, sodomy, sexual inversion, and intersexuality in 1938. San Domino was the only island in the Tremiti island chain where all the exiles were homosexual however a number of homosexual men were interned along with political prisoners on other small islands in the chain, such as Ustica.

In a semi-anonymous account of this time by someone who let himself be known as Giuseppe B. noted that "In those days if you were a *femminella* (a slang Italian word for a gay

man) you couldn't even leave your home, or
make yourself noticed - the police would arrest
you...On the island, on the other hand, we would
celebrate our Saint's days or the arrival of
someone new." Overnight they would be locked
into their barracks, on San Domino it was said
that they were locked in at 8 pm to be released
at 8 am. To keep themselves entertained
Giuseppe B. stated that they "...did theatre, and
we could dress as women there and no one
would say anything." However, after the outbreak
of World War II the Tremiti islands were needed
for other instances of internment, concluding
their exile in June of 1940 to return to mainland
Italy and conclude their sentence in house arrest
(*ammonizione*) in the places they had come
from.

In the 2004 documentary "Ricordare"
(*Remember*), director Gabriella Roman
interviewed various homosexual Italiains who
were all kept anonymous. In an interview with a
man referred to as Giovanni he reflects on his

time at Ustica saying that unlike the prisoners at San Domino, at Ustica they were locked in their barracks at 6 pm in the summer and 4 pm in the winter but similarly to San Domino, they entertained themselves by doing theater performances. When asked to speak about his experience there he stated:

> I recall Ustica's beauty due to my love for the sea. The abundance of dogs there brought me immense joy, overshadowing any other concerns. Leaving filled me with genuine regret; I wished to prolong my stay. Upon our departure, the Americans granted us freedom, and I returned to Naples, where my partner and I established a boutique via in Chiaia.

Benadusi, Lorenzo, Suzanne Dingee, and Jennifer Pudney. The Enemy of the New Man: Homosexuality in

Fascist Italy. Madison, WI: The University of Wisconsin Press, 2012.

Blamires, Cyprian P., Cyprian Blamires, and Paul Jackson. World Fascism: A Historical Encyclopedia. 1. Vol. 1. ABC-CLIO, 2006.

Ebner, Michael R. "The Persecution of Homosexual Men under Fascism." Essay. In Gender, Family, and Sexuality., edited by P. Wilson. London: Palgrave Macmillan, 2004.

Garofalo, Piero, Elizabeth Leake, and Dana Renga . Story. In Internal Exile in Fascist Italy: History and Representations of Confino. Manchester University Press, 2022.

Johnston, Alan. "A Gay Island Community Created by Italy's Fascists." BBC News. BBC, June 12, 2013.

CHAPTER THREE

GERMANY

At the Paleolithic site at Gonnersdorf, a German site on the banks of the Rhine, archaeologists have uncovered dozens of plaques showing couples of women including a 12,000 years old carving titled *The Dancers* that shows two females rubbing their breasts in an affectionate attitude.

When looking at the scientific origins of the word "homosexual" (specifying "scientific" because the word has been used earlier than its scientific origins in personal letters, the earliest of which is from 1868) the first scientific work in which the word "homosexual" comes up is in *Psychopathia Sexualis* by psychologist Richard Von Krafft-Ebing, published in 1886 in Germany. In this work, he also brought terminology such as Sadist, Masochist, Bisexual, Necrophilia, etc. It is important to keep in mind that these behaviors existed before the word and we had a legislature in place to regulate and control those who did not fit into the status quo.

In the German Criminal code from May 15th, 1871 to March 10th, 1994, Section 175 read; "Unnatural sexual acts (*Widernäturliche Unzucht*) committed between persons of the male sex, or by humans with animals, is punishable with imprisonment; a loss of civil rights may also be sentenced." In 1907, a Reichstag Committee decided to broaden the paragraph to make lesbian sexual acts punishable as well, however, this did not pass.

Despite the criminal code in place, there were some medical professionals who had a progressive mindset such as Dr. Magnus Hirschfeld, a gay, Jewish, German physician specializing in sexual health. He contrasted the new theories in psychology stating that those fitting outside of the gender binary and heterosexuality were of ill mental health, instead, he supported the idea of a "third sex" (*Geschlecht*) and that a spectrum of sexuality existed for all gender identities including the idea that transgender people could be straight, a sentiment that is lost on some people today and that transgender patients should have access to gender-affirming care. In early 1919 he purchased a Berlin villa and opened the Institute for Sexual Research (*Institut für Sexualwissenschaft*) and by 1930 the institute would perform the first modern gender-affirmation surgery.

In 1935 the Nazis redefined the crime as a felony and thus increased the maximum penalty from six months to five years imprisonment because Hitler saw gay men as a hindrance in his campaign to purify Germany because their partnerships could not bear children who would grow the Aryan race. However, as early as May 1933 the Nazis publicly condemned homosexuality allowing National Socialist students to ransack the Hirschfeld's Institute. In 1936 the Reich Central Office for Combating Homosexuality and Abortion was set up by Heinrich Himmler, a leading member of the Nazi party. Those found guilty of homosexual acts were identified by inverted pink triangles (*die Rosa-Winkel*) just as Jewish people wore a yellow Star of David on their uniforms. Concentration camps tended to be segregated and homosexual men were frequently used for medical experimentation to find cures for typhus fever or homosexuality, which included experiments such as injecting them with testosterone to see if it would make them straight, and many of them underwent forced sterilization by castration. In 1942 Himmler pledged to "eliminate" homosexuality from Germany in a speech and death was introduced as a penalty for homosexuality.

Germany has many stories of how the second world war affected queer people however for the sake of brevity this section focuses on a representative on each side of the coin; Ernst Röhm, a military officer, part of the Storm Troopers (*Sturmabteilung* or *SA*) who described himself as "same-sex oriented" (*gleichgeschlechtlich*) and Anne Frank, a Jewish child who fled with her family from Germany to the Netherlands to go into hiding from Nazi persecution, and though she did not identify herself as such, from her diary she is believed to have been bisexual.

Ernst Röhm

Ernst Julius Günther Röhm was born on November 28th, 1887 in Munich, Germany. On July 23rd, 1906, Röhm joined the Royal Bavarian 10th Infantry Regiment of the German Imperial Army as a cadet despite his family having no military tradition and he would become a commissioned officer on March 12th, 1908.

In August of 1914, at the outbreak of World War I, Röhm was assigned to assist the commanding officer of the 1st Battalion, 10th Infantry Regiment with unit administration. In

September he suffered from a severe facial wound that would physically scar him for the rest of his life. He was promoted to first lieutenant (*Oberleutnant*) in April 1915. During the battle in June of 1916, he sustained a serious chest wound for which he was awarded the Iron Cross First Class and spent the remainder of the war in France and Romania as a staff officer and was promoted to captain (*Hauptmann*) in April 1917.

Röhm would become a member of the German Workers' Party which formed just after World War I however this group would be short-lived, from being founded on January 5th, 1919 until February 24th, 1920 but the group would become the precursor of the Nazi Party of which Röhm would become an early member as a military officer and part of the Storm Troopers (*Sturmabteilung* or *SA*) and becoming a close friend and early ally of Adolf Hitler which was interesting as he openly opposed a penal code Hitler intended to uphold, Section 175: Unnatural sexual acts (*Widernäturliche Unzucht*) as by the mid-1920's Röhm was not secretive about his sexual orientation. Röhm believed that the Nazi homosocial (*Männerbund*) views that organizations should hold a standard of discipline and resolve to overcome the threat of chaos and ambivalence, walked a fluid line with homosexuality.

This was not the only point Röhm and Hitler disagreed on, Röhm wanted the SA to absorb or supplant the German Army (*Reichswehr*) however Hitler disagreed until 1930 when Hitler requested Röhm return from Bolivia to reorganize the SA. SA intimidation contributed to the rise of the Nazi party however their reputation for the violent suppression of rival parties during electoral campaigns and heavy drinking was a hindrance to their rise to power, as was the rumored homosexuality of Röhm and other SA leaders such as his deputy Edmund Heines. In June 1931, the *Münchener Post* began attacking Röhm and the SA regarding homosexuality in its ranks and then in March

1932, the paper obtained and published some private letters of his in which Röhm described himself as "same-sex oriented" (*gleichgeschlechtlich*). Hitler was aware of Röhm's homosexuality. Their friendship is shown as Röhm remained one of the few allowed to use the familiar German form of "you" (*du)* when conversing with Hitler.

After a failed attempt to run for presidential office, in January of 1933 Adolf Hitler was appointed to the position of chancellor under Paul von Hindenburg. During this time Röhm was considered by Hitler for a position in his cabinet but was convinced otherwise by other members of the SA. Röhm and Heines' homosexuality had at this point proved convenient for Hitler during the upcoming purge of SA leaders, as it could tie him and others to the Night of the Long Knives (*Röhm Putsch*), a fictional coup which was said to take place from June 30th to July 2nd of 1934. They would be executed on June 30th, 1934,

Hitler gave Röhm the choice to commit suicide, which he refused.

When Hindenburg passed away on August 2nd 1934 the positions of chancellor and president combined resulting in Hitler rising to the position of "Leader" (*Führer*) and the Nazi Party gained control over Germany.

Anne Frank

Annelies Marie Frank was born on June 12th, 1929 in Frankfurt, Germany to Jewish parents Otto and Edith Frank and older sister Margot.

When Hindenburg passed away on August 2nd 1934 and the positions of chancellor and president were combined promoting Hitler to "Leader" (*Führer*), the Frank family moved to Amsterdam, Netherlands. There Otto founded a company that initially traded in pectin, a fiber found in fruits used as a thickener in cooking and baking and eventually expanded to selling herbs and spices in addition.

On September 1st, 1939, Nazi Germany invaded Poland, kickstarting the Second World War. By May 10th, 1940, the Nazis invaded the Netherlands, with the Dutch army surrendering on the 15th the Nazis introduced laws and regulations singling out the Jewish populus including excluding them from parks, cinemas, or non-Jewish shops, however Jewish people were also not allowed to run their own businesses, meaning Otto lost his company and eventually, in 1941, the Franks and many other Jewish families would become stateless, with the loss of their German citizenship.

On July 6th, 1942, ten days before they had planned to go into hiding, they had a change of plans due to the notice Edith received to report for relocation to the work camp. They concealed themselves in a set of rooms behind a three-shelf, timber bookcase built by Johannes Voskuijl in the building where Otto had worked.

From behind that bookcase, Frank kept a diary she called "Kitty", a red and white checkered autograph book, she had received for her 13th birthday present as she strived to be a journalist when she grew up. On April 5th, 1944 she wrote:

> *I'm overjoyed that at least I can write. And if I don't have the talent to write books or newspaper articles, I can always write for myself. But I want to achieve more than that. I can't imagine having to live like Mother, Mrs. van Daan, and all the women who go about their work and are then forgotten. I need to have something besides a husband and children to devote myself to! I don't want to have lived in vain like most people. I want to be useful or bring enjoyment to all people, even those I've never met. I want to go on living even after my death! And that's why I'm so grateful to God*

for having given me this gift, which
I can use to develop myself and to
express all that's inside me!

Though this diary was a wonderful insight into daily life for the Jewish population in German-occupied spaces, this also gave an insight into Frank's mind. Frank never uses terminology to identify herself as part of the LGBTQ+ community however inferences can be made from the curiosity displayed in excerpts from her diary such as that from January 6th, 1944 while she reminisces of a time before the attic:

> *Once, while staying at Jacque's, my*
> *curiosity about her hidden body*
> *became overwhelming. I had never*
> *seen it before. I proposed that, as a*
> *gesture of friendship, we touch each*
> *other's breasts. Jacque declined. I*
> *also felt a strong urge to kiss her,*
> *which I acted upon. Whenever I*
> *encounter a female nude, like the*

Venus in my art history book, I am
filled with ecstasy. Their beauty is
sometimes so overwhelming that it
brings tears to my eyes. If only I
had a girlfriend!

However, Anne would continue to have a romance with Peter van Pels, another in hiding behind that bookcase. On July 13th 1942, the Franks were joined by the van Pels family, made up of Hermann, Auguste, and 16-year-old Peter, and then in November by Fritz Pfeffer. On the first day he kisses her she writes: "Remember yesterday's date, since it was a red-letter day for me. Isn't it an important day for every girl when she gets her first kiss?"

The family would be arrested from behind their bookcase by a group of German uniformed police (*Grüne Polizei*) led by SS-Oberscharführer Karl Silberbauer of the Sicherheitsdienst on August 4th, 1944. How the German uniformed police found the family is still speculated. In 2015 it was theorized that Nelly, the daughter of

Johannes Voskuijl, was the informer as she had moved back to Amsterdam in 1943 after running away with a Nazi Officer, in her nephew's biography he speculated it was her based on her being an Nazi informer from the ages of 19 to 23 and the SS Officer who took the report noted that the informer had "the voice of a young woman". In 2016, the Anne Frank House launched an investigation centering on ration card fraud instead however this did not rule out a betrayal. This allowed an investigation to begin in January 2022 about Arnold van den Bergh, a member of Amsterdam's Jewish Council postulating that van den Bergh gave up the Franks to save his family after the publication of The Betrayal of Anne Frank by Rosemary Sullivan, claiming that the Amsterdam Jewish council had a list of Jewish hiding places.

The Franks, van Pelses, and Pfeffer were taken to RSHA headquarters, where they were interrogated and held until August 5th when they were transferred to the House of Detention (*Huis van Bewaring)* and two days later transported to the Westerbork transit camp, where they were sent to the Punishment Barracks for hard labor as they were considered criminals for being arrested in hiding. On November 1st, 1944, Anne and her sister, Margot, were transferred from Auschwitz to Bergen-Belsen concentration camp, where they died a few months later. It was speculated that they had succumbed to typhus and the Red Cross originally estimated that they had to have died in March, with Dutch authorities setting March 31st as the official date. Later research has suggested they died in February or early March.

Frank's father, Otto, would first publish an abridged version of her diary on June 25th, 1947. In this version, where 30% of the original text was excluded, including the sections regarding sexuality. In 1995, "The Definitive Edition" was published, adding back the lost sections of the diary including sections that were later rewritten by Frank when she was fifteen as she had changed her perspective on her mother and sister after being used to the close quarters they had had to exist in together. She was able to go on living after her death as she had hoped as today her diary remains one of the few detailed, first-hand accounts of Jewish life during German occupation.

Berenbaum, Michael, Abraham J. Peck, and R. Lautman. "The Pink Triangle: Homosexuals as 'Enemies of the State'." Essay. In The Holocaust and History: The Known, the Unknown, the Disputed and the Re-Examined.Bloomington, IN: Indiana University Press, 1998.

Blamires, Cyprian P., Cyprian Blamires, and Paul Jackson. World Fascism: A Historical Encyclopedia. 1. Vol. 1.ABC-CLIO, 2006. Ebner, Michael R. "The Persecution of Homosexual Men under Fascism." Essay. In Gender, Family, and Sexuality., edited by P. Wilson. London: Palgrave Macmillan, 2004.

Frank, Anne, Mirjam Pressler, Susan Massotty, and Nadia Murad. The Diary of a Young Girl: The DefinitiveEdition. New York: Anchor Books, a division of Penguin Random House LLC, 2022.

Hancock, Eleanor. Ernst Röhm: Hitler's SA chief of staff. Basingstoke: Palgrave Macmillan, 2008.

Heger, H. "The Men with the Pink Triangle." Men's Press, 1986.

Papirblat, Shlomo. "Has Anne Frank's Betrayer Been Found?" Haaretz.com, April 8, 2015.

Schillace, Brandy. "The Forgotten History of the World's First Trans Clinic." Scientific American, March 6, 2023.

Wills, Matthew. "Ernst Röhm, the Highest-Ranking Gay Nazi - JSTOR DAILY." JSTOR, March 27, 2017.

ALLIED POWERS

CHAPTER FOUR

FRANCE

Dating back to the Paleolithic period, evidence of homosexuality, specifically female homosexuality can be found by looking at Laussel rock shelter, the same site the discovery of Venus of Laussel, a goddess figure, a popular motif in Paleolithic art, depicting a woman with exaggerated breasts and hips, they also found carvings of two women with their legs intertwined, in the posture known as scissoring, dating about 27,000 years ago and stone plaque engravings found in a cave in the La Marche county of France, depicting cunnilingus between two women and anal intercourse between two men.

During the *Ancien régime* sodomy was punishable by death, the last people to be put to death on July 6th, 1750 were Jean Diot and

Bruno Lenoir by were burned to death for behaving "in an indecent and reprehensible manner". The first French Revolution decriminalized homosexuality when the Penal Code of 1791, though homosexuality and cross-dressing continued to be widely viewed as being immoral.

Though homosexuality and cross-dressing were seen as immoral by society, France still had an unrecognized homosexual culture. In 1924, the first French magazine for homosexuals, *Inversions*, was founded; however after the publication of their fourth issue it ceased publication in early 1925 due to persistent persecution.

The regions of Alsace and Lorraine were annexed by Nazi Germany after they invaded Paris on June 14th, 1940 which led France to sign an armistice on the 22nd. During this time those persecuted of LGBTQ+ crimes were interned in concentration camps, additionally, those in unaffected regions were persecuted under the Vichy Regime, the government established a regime in an unoccupied "free zone" (*zone libre*), where it remained responsible for the civil administration of France as well as its colonies, despite there being no laws criminalizing homosexuality.

As the Nazi regime began overtaking France various queer people calling France home made efforts to work against the Axis forces. These people included Ovida Delect, a transgender woman who established a resistance group with the intention of creating major disturbances by disseminating fake news amongst the ranks of the National Popular Youth and Josephine Baker, a bisexual, American born performer who helped the *France libre* (Free French) movement by carrying sensitive information to the Allied forces under the guise of touring for her show.

Ovida Delect

Ovida Delect was born Jean-Pierre Voidies, on October 9th, 1926 in Caen, France. According to Victoria Thérame, who wrote the preface to Delect's first part of her two part biography, *La vocation d'être femme, itinéraire d'une transsexuelle vécue* (The vocation of being a woman: Itinerary of a lived transsexuality), Delect was: "...a kid who has a kid's body and ... a sixteen year old boy who knows he is a girl,"

In the early 1940s, Delect was a student at the *Lycée* (second and last stage of secondary education in the French educational system) *Malherbe* at the University of Caen. There she established a small resistance group against the German occupation of France with a number of other students including Roger Câtel, Bernard Duval, Bernard Boulot, Claude Lunois and Jean-Paul Mérouze. They pretended to be members of the National Popular Youth, a branch of the National Popular Rally, presenting as supporters of collaboration with the Germans. In

her time masquerading as a National Popular
Youth member, Delect managed to steal
important files and create major disturbances in
the ranks of this organization by disseminating
fake news items and false information. These
actions led to her and several of her comrades
to be arrested by the Gestapo on February 23rd,
1944 at the age of 17. She was tortured for at
least ten days, before being deported to
Germany and imprisoned at the Neuengamme
concentration camp but under torture, she did
not denounce her comrades.

	After the war, Delect returned to her
studies and obtained her second baccalaureate in
1946 and began to publish her resistance poems
in local journals winning her the Paul Valéry Prize
in 1946, the year after Paul Valéry, the twelve
time Nobel Prize nominee for Literature and one
of her works was read at the Maison de la
Mutualité in Paris and soon after she left Caen to
study in Paris, where she formed a circle of
poets. To survive in Paris, she worked at what

she described as "small jobs" until she passed the entrance exam to the *École normale supérieure* (School of Civil Servants or *normaliens*) and became a literature teacher.

During the summer of 1952 in Hyères, she met her future wife Huguette Voidies, a kindergarten teacher from Sarthe. While she did not yet go by the name Ovida publicly, she confided her identity to her friends and wife but in 1953, Ovida read about the transition of Christine Jorgensen in the press and was reportedly shocked by the similarity between their lives.

At the beginning of the 1960s, Delect, under her birth name Jean-Pierre Voidies, became mayor of Freneuse, a town of 2,800 inhabitants west of Paris. During this time she and her wife had a son together, Jean-Noel in 1966.

At the end of the 1960s, Delect wrote *La Demoiselle de Kerk* (The Young Lady of Caen), a poetic prose novel that tells the story of a young girl under the occupation in Caen. She commented that the work was "a transposed autobiography". In 1975 she began writing under the pen name Olivia Ovida Delect and in 1981 she retired from teaching and politics at the age of 55 and began making her social transition, choosing to publicly go by her pen name.

In 1986 Delect elected to participate in the filming of a documentary directed by Françoise Romand, her third of now twenty-six documentaries, called *Appelez-moi Madame* (Call Me Madame) highlighting Delect's life from her role in WWII, being the author of over 40 books and her sex change.

Delect died on October 9th 1996. In June 2019, Paris named a square Ovida Delect square for her.

Josephine Baker

Freda Josephine McDonald was born June 3rd, 1906 in St. Louis, Missouri to Carrie McDonald and a father whose identity is contested however her mother later married Arthur Martin, with whom she had a son and two more daughters based on the 1920 census numbers, causing Josephine to take up work doing laundry as a live-in domestic worker at the age of eight where she was abused by her white employers by burning her hands when she used too much soap. Baker was eleven when the East St. Louis massacre occurred on May 28th and from July 1st through 3rd, 1917 in which a series of attacks against African Americans occurred displacing an estimated 6,000 African American residents, this combined with complications with her mother, who did not encourage her dreams of becoming an entertainer, led Baker to live in the slums of St. Louis, sleeping in cardboard shelters, scavenging for food in garbage cans. In 1918 she dropped out of school at age twelve, dancing on a street corner to make ends meet eventually joining the St. Louis Chorus vaudeville act and began waitressing at the 'Old Chauffeur's

Club' at the age of thirteen. It was here she met Willie Wells, who she married within that year.

Due to her integration into the nightlife scene, in 1920 she met Clara Smith, the second most recorded blues singer of the 1920s while performing in St. Louis. At this point Baker had separated from her husband and took up a short lived relationship with Smith while they were both in St Louis.

Her marriage lasted less than a year as she moved to Following her divorce from Wells, moved to New York City to perform at the Plantation Club and she found additional work with a street performance group called the Jones Family Band. By 1921, Baker had remarried at the age of fifteen to William Howard Baker from whom she would gain the last name she would use for the rest of her performing career. Baker soon landed a role in the chorus line of the show "Shuffle Along" which traveled with a US touring company. Though Baker was often on the road she frequently returned with gifts and money for her mother and younger half-sister though she struggled to have a healthy relationship with her mother, who opposed her becoming an entertainer and scolded her for not tending to her husband. Eventually "Shuffle Along" was brought to Broadway where she remained until the show closed in 1923 though her Broadway career would not end there, Baker was cast in the chorus line in the show "The Chocolate Dandies" which opened on September 1st, 1924, but as larger career opportunities brought her to France, she left the show before its closing in November of that year.

In 1925 Baker sailed to Paris, arriving in time to open in the musical "la Revue nègre" at *Théâtre des Champs-Élysées* where she met Ada "Bricktop" Smith and they bonded over their shared experience of being two of the few people of color from the US to move to Paris adding her to the list of many flings Baker would have in 1925 including Belgian novelist Georges Simenon despite being married until later in the year. She became instantly successful for the eroticism in her dancing landing her a tour of her show throughout Europe, however this tour would be cut short in 1926 as Baker chose to break her contract to come back to Paris to star at the *Folies Bergère*. By 1929 she would go on tour again, becoming the first African-American star to visit Yugoslavia, despite donating a portion of the show's proceeds to poor children in Serbia, she was met with disdain in Croatia with the influence of clergy and morality police canceling some of her shows.

Despite her success in Europe when she attempted to return to the US in 1936 for the revival of the show "Ziegfeld Follies" on Broadway the show was not as successful. "Time" magazine referred to her as a "Negro wench ... whose dancing and singing might be topped anywhere outside of Paris", she was soon replaced by Gypsy Rose Lee. When she returned to Paris in 1937, she married the French industrialist Jean Lion, and became a French citizen while giving up her American citizenship in the process.

In 1939 Baker met Frida Kahlo who had traveled to Paris to put on an art exhibition, the two were rumored to have a short affair in the time Kahlo was in Paris. In September, when France declared war on Germany in response to the invasion of Poland, Baker was recruited by the *Deuxième Bureau de l'État-major général* (Second Bureau of the General Staff) which was France's external military intelligence agency, as an "honorable correspondent" to work with the head of French counterintelligence in Paris, Jacques Abtey. As she was a well known entertainer it did not raise suspicion when she socialized with the Germans at ministries, night clubs, and embassies, including the Italian embassy, to secretly gather information.

When the Germans invaded France in 1940, Baker fled Paris to south France where she began renting Château des Milandes where she housed people interested in supporting the

France libre (Free French) effort led by Charles de Gaulle who supplied them with visas. The Deuxième Bureau was dissolved in 1940 upon the armistice with Germany however as an entertainer, Baker was able to continue moving around Europe carrying information written in invisible ink on sheet music to England, about airfields, harbors, and German troop concentrations in the West of France.

In 1941, she and her entourage went to the French colonies in North Africa. From a base in Morocco, she made tours of Spain supplying the Allied powers with notes with the information from the North African campaign she gathered she kept pinned inside her underwear. After having another of many miscarriages, though this was also speculated to be a stillborn birth, Baker developed an infection that led to sepsis, requiring a hysterectomy. After her recovery, she started touring to entertain British, French, and American soldiers in North Africa, as the *France libre* had no organized entertainment network for their troops, Baker and her entourage managed for the most part on their own.

After the war, Baker was awarded the Resistance Medal by the French Committee of National Liberation, the *Croix de Guerre* (War Cross) by the French military, and was named a *Chevalier of the Légion d'honneur* (National Order of the Legion of Honour) by General Charles de Gaulle. She then returned to the *Folies Bergère* with great success.

In 1951, Baker was invited back to the US for a nightclub engagement in Miami but only after winning a public battle over desegregating the club's audience after turning down a $10,000 bribe made by the nightclub. Baker followed up her sold-out run at the club with a national tour, however this would not be the end of her run-is with racial discrimination in her stint in the US. When she arrived in New York with her husband, French composer and conductor Jo Bouillon, they were refused reservations at 36 different hotels. This led her to write several articles about segregation in the United States and give a talk at Fisk University, a historically black college in Nashville, Tennessee, on "France, North Africa and the Equality of the Races in France". Her tour was soon cut short when at the Stork Club in Manhattan in October 1951 Baker criticized the club's unwritten policy of discouraging Black patrons, Walter Winchell, a broadway and gossip columnist accused Baker of harboring Communist sympathies resulting in the termination of Baker's work visa but not until after Baker was hired to crown the Queen of the Cavalcade of Jazz for the famed eighth Cavalcade of Jazz concert held at Wrigley Field in Los Angeles on June 1st, 1952.

During her participation in the civil rights movement, Baker began to adopt children which she referred to as "The Rainbow Tribe" as they were all of different ethnicities. This included two daughters, French-born Marianne and Moroccan-born Stellina, and ten sons, Japanese-born Janot (born Teruya) and Akio,

Colombian-born Luis, Finnish-born Jari, French-born Jean-Claude, Noël, and Moïse, Algerian-born Brahim, Ivorian-born Koffi, and Venezuelan-born Mara.

In 1968, Baker lost her château in southern France due to her unpaid debts and was offered an apartment in Roquebrune by Princess Grace of Monaco. Baker was sporadically back on stage including doing shows at the Olympia in Paris in 1968, in Belgrade and at Carnegie Hall in 1973 and at the Royal Variety Performance at the London Palladium and at the "Gala du Cirque" in Paris in 1974.

On April 8th, 1975, Baker starred in a retrospective revue at the Bobino in Paris, "*Joséphine à Bobino 1975*" (Josephine at Bobino 1975) to celebrate her 50 years in show business. The demand for seating was so high that fold-out chairs had to be added to accommodate spectators. For the opening-night showing, the audience included names such as Mick Jagger, Diana Ross and Liza Minnelli. Four days later, Baker was found in a coma in her bed surrounded by newspapers with glowing reviews of her performance after suffering a cerebral hemorrhage. She was taken to Pitié-Salpêtrière Hospital, where she died, aged 68, on April 12th, 1975.

Ansede, Manuel. "Los Gays Paleolíticos Salen de La Caverna." Público, August 4, 2010.

Delect, Ovida. La Vocation d'Etre Femme itinéraire d'une transsexualité vécue. Paris: Editions l'Harmattan, 1996. Jones, Sherry.

Josephine Baker's last dance. Thorndike Press, 2019.

Matthews, Dasha. "The Activism of Josephine Baker - UMKC Women's Center." UMKC Women's Center - Advancing gender equity, February 26, 2018.

CHAPTER FIVE

UNITED KINGDOM

Prior to the introduction of Christianity to Britain in 597 AD, it is likely that homosexuality was practiced freely based on how it was dealt with in the church; however, no surviving Celtic written records have survived. Not until 1533 was homosexuality categorized as illegal as opposed to just sinful with the passing of the Buggery Act where male anal sex was made punishable by death. This was the country's first civil sodomy law, proceedings were previously taken up in the ecclesiastical courts. Legal restriction regarding sex between women was never addressed.

From 1805 and 1835 England hanged 55 men for being found guilty of the Buggery Act however in 1861 section 61 of the Offences

Against the Person Act lessened the penalty for the Buggery Act from death to imprisonment. The extent of what could get charged was extended to include any homosexual act with or without a witness as opposed to just sodomy in with the Labouchere Amendment or the "oath clause" which was section 11 of the Criminal Law Amendment Act of 1885. With this amendment letters between two men expressing affection were known to be enough evidence to convict, an example of this is the case of Oscar Wilde who in 1892 popularized wearing a green carnation as a gay symbol as he instructed his friends to wear them on their lapels to the opening of his comedy, *Lady Windermere's Fan*. Subsequently, the green carnation became a coded symbol that a man was attracted to men, and Wilde, as a symbol in his own right, was sentenced to two years of penal labor from 1895 to 1897. Though this act specified acts made between males it was made ambiguous with the term "gross indecency" and was extended to be used against women, specifically in the military stripping them of their metals.

Despite the cultural and political injustice faced by queer people in the United Kingdom there were still people who believed that education was the most powerful tactic in the second world war. Specifically Evelyn Irons, a lesbian Journalist who was among the first to reach newly liberated Paris and first woman journalist to reach Hitler's *Obersalzberg* (Eagle's Nest) and Alan Turing, a gay mathematician behind cracking the Enigma code on German U-boats.

Evelyn Irons

Evelyn Graham Irons was born on June 17th, 1900 in Glasgow, Scotland to Joseph Jones Irons, a stockbroker, and Edith Mary Latta.

She studied at Somerville College, one of two womens colleges at Oxford University after which she landed a job in journalism working for *The Daily Mail*. Initially, the editor assigned her to the beauty page, despite the fact that Irons had never worn makeup. In 1931, Irons went to interview Vita Sackville-West, the successful novelist, poet and journalist after her novel The Edwardians had become a best-seller, at Sissinghurst Castle Garden in Kent, England where she was designing and shaping the famous gardens. Sackville-West was married to Harold Nicolson at the time however she had already had several extra-marital affairs, while Irons was involved with Olive Rinder who Irons was living with at the time in their apartment in Chelsea, however Rinder also became a lover of Sackville-West, forming a menage-a-trois during 1932 that ended when Irons met a fellow journalist, Joy McSweeney at a party in July, 1931.

Eventually Irons would be fired from *The Daily Mail* for "looking unfashionable" and she found employment elsewhere at the *Evening Standard* where she edited the "women's interest" pages until 1939 when World War II broke out. She informed the news editor "From now on I'm working for you." Though General Montgomery, commander of the British Eighth Army, objected to women reporters on the battlefield, she gained the support of French General Jean de Lattre de Tassigny and became one of the first journalists to reach newly liberated Paris on August 19th, 1944. She was the first woman journalist to reach Hitler's *Obersalzberg* (Eagle's Nest) after its capture on May 2nd, 1945 where after climbing there through the snow she reportedly helped herself to a bottle of Hitler's "excellent Rhine wine".

After the war Irons would continue to cover political news, her most notable assignments included traveling to the United States in 1952 to cover the presidential election and when the CIA operation to overthrow Jacobo Árbenz, code-named Operation PBSuccess, was authorized by Eisenhower in August 1953. In 1954 she broke a news embargo on the overthrow of Guatemalan President Jacobo

Arbenz Guzmán by hiring a mule to take her to Chiquimula, Guatemala while other journalists, forbidden to cross the border, were forced to wait in Honduras. She became the first reporter to reach the headquarters of the Provisional Government.

After her assignment in 1952 she elected to stay in the US, settling near Brewster, New York with McSweeney where they rented the cottage to several tenants, including the American cookbook writer Sylvia Vaughn Thompson. Irons and McSweeney lived together until McSweeney's death in 1978 or 1988, sources vary. Irons died in Brewster, New York, on April 3rd, 2000, two months short of her 100th birthday.

Alan Turing

Alan Turing was born on June 23rd, 1912 in London, England, and was privately educated throughout his upbringing. He then attended Sherborne School beginning in May 1926 where he met who he credited with being his first love, Christopher Morcom. One reminiscent thought of Christoper read "There were times when I felt his personality particularly strongly, at present, I'm thinking of an evening when he was waiting outside the labs and when I came to he grasped me with his big hand and took me out to see the stars."

Christopher was introduced to him by his older brother Rupert Morcom. Christopher was a year above Turing, attending Sherborne School beginning in May 1925. The Morcoms came from a legacy of steam, steam engines via their grandfather, and steam turbines via their father within the company of Bellis and Morcom in Birmingham, founded in 1852. His mother was the daughter of Sir Joseph Swan, the inventor of the electric light in 1879. Their financial gains led to the ability to build Christopher a laboratory at home which is where their shared interests began, with discussing chemical experiments with Turing's favorite solution, iodine. He had described it as "...a beautiful experiment, two solutions are mixed in a beaker, and after waiting for some very definite period, the whole suddenly becomes a deep blue. I have known it to take a time, thirty seconds, and then turn blue in one-tenth of a second or less." From this Christopher and Turing went on to attempt to find a relation between the time and the concentration of solutions to verify Rupert's theories regarding the time delay. Unfortunately, they went on to prove Rupert's theories wrong however this encouraged Turing to configure his theories and continue writing to Christopher regarding this during breaks when they were apart as well as notes to each other during classes.

In 1929 both Christopher and Turing took on the ambitious task of applying for an open scholarship at Trinity College, Cambridge, slightly more ambitious on the side of Turing at the age of 17 in an attempt not to lose Christopher for a year. They would take the train to London to visit

Trinity College, staying in the dorms and making acquaintances with other budding intellectuals. During this time Turing would test Christopher by walking separately from him and wait for Christopher to ask Turing to walk beside him, as he knew Turing held affection for him.

On December 18th, the results were published in the *Times* showing that Christopher had been awarded the scholarship however Turing had not. During the holiday break Turing would write Christopher multiple times, one of which regarding where else he should apply, to which Christopher replied that he would prefer Turing try again and join him at Trinity. Christopher was to have gone into residency in October 1930 however on February 6th of 1930 he succumbed to bovine tuberculosis after being taken to London to undergo two operations, Turing was unaware that he had had previous operations due to his condition in 1927.

In the letter he wrote to Christopher's mother on the 8th, the day of Christopher's

funeral, Turing expressed "Although that interest
(in their shared research) is partly gone, I know I
must put as much energy, if not as much interest
into my work as if he were alive because that is
what he would like me to do." His family had sent
a picture of Christopher to Turing, who reported
back saying that he kept it on his desk and
Christopher reminded him to work hard, the
Morcoms invited Turing on a trip to Spain taking
Christoper's place during their break at the end
of April. He opened up to Mrs. Morcom during
this time about how he felt attracted to
Christopher before he had gotten to know him.
Upon his return, Mrs. Morcom invited Turing to
accompany her to Christopher's laboratory to
sort through his things, many of which she
allowed him to bring home with him as
keepsakes of Christopher, shortly after Mrs.
Turing wrote to Mrs. Morcom stating that Turing
was treasuring these keepsakes "...with the
tenderness of a woman."

The Morcoms would begin the Christopher Morcom Prize for Science in Christopher's memory, which Turing would be the first (and second in 1931) to win. For his prize, he chose a book titled "Mathematical Recreations and Essays"

Turing was uninterested in making other friends in his year, however, he met someone three years his junior named Victor Beuttell. Originally, he was drawn to him when he found out Beutell's mother was dying of bovine tuberculosis. They spent free time toying with codes and ciphers stemming from the last chapter of the book Turing won for his Morcom Prize which focused on cryptography. Turing went a route different from mathematics with his ciphers, poking holes in a piece of paper for Beuttell to page through books to find the specific page Turing used to create his cipher in order to crack it.

In 1931 Turing began his academic work at the University of Cambridge to study mathematics at King's College, after failing again to obtain the Trinity Scholarship. King's College was described as a "ghetto of sexual descent" which gave Turing the freedom to express his ideas and feelings though he was hindered by the potential of being perceived as a "pansy". The first known use of pansies to describe homosexual love between men was in Marcel Proust's *Sodome et Gomorrhe* (Sodom and Gomorrah) published in 1921 referred to male-male courtship as being similar to the process of flower fertilization in which men were called "evening botanists," "buttercups," or "horticultural lads."

As was the case with his previous schooling, Turing was less than interested in making friends, he had one colleague with whom he would attend lectures with however it seemed that was the extent of their friendship. There were a handful of instances in which Turing expressed his feelings for those he befriended such as Kenneth Harrison who did not reciprocate his feelings, James Adkins and Fred Clayton, with whom he would take part in casual sexual relationships, however, he was not comfortable expressing his sexuality. Despite this, his homosexuality was not a secret to those from his previous school as shown by one incident in December 1933 at the Founders Feist where a former classmate mocked Turing by saying "Don't look at me like that, I'm not a homosexual." to which Turing responded: "If you want to go to bed it'll be one-sided."

Turing graduated in 1934 and was elected to one of forty-six fellows at Kings College to research probability theory. Before beginning his fellowship he took a cycling trip to Germany with Dennis Williams, a first-year student from moral sciences. Unlike Turing, Williams felt it necessary to conform to the local customs, as they were surrounded by Nazi flags, and would give his salutations with "Heil Hitler", getting him in physical scraps in at least one instance as he said it to a socialist who was staying in their hostel. During their trip, a news article came out about the assassination of Ernst Röhm, after being given the opportunity to commit suicide and Röhm refusing to do so for being a "homosexual traitor".

His fellowship was to last three years, he was given a stipend however he supplemented his income as an advisor to undergraduates. In 1935, Turing started to consider how to solve David Hilbert's Decision Problem (*Entscheidungsproblem*) posted in 1928 in which the question is posed; can we decide if any statement posed in mathematics is true or false? As mathematical symbols are given a predetermined value, Turing looked into the mechanical rules of mathematics considering the typewriter as they worked by manipulating symbols and did so in a way that the operator could be completely certain of the outcome of each key, however, they could not do so without human intervention and they could only write the symbols, therefore Turing dreamt up a "super-typewriter" that could operate without intervention. In 1936 he published a paper *On Computable Numbers, with an Application to the Entscheidungsproblem [Decision Problem]* where he postulated that the answer to Hilbert's question was no, there was no definite method to solve all mathematical problems due to the inconsistency of "uncomputable" numbers. This paper caught the attention of Alonzo Church, who had published a paper that reached the same conclusion as Turing but with a different method, the Turing method that would be integral in the impending science of computing. When comprehending the similarities of the paper, Max Newman, a mathematics lecturer at Cambridge sent a letter to Church asking him to arrange for Turing to work with him at Princeton as a proctor fellow. Only one proctor fellowship per year was allotted for a representative at Cambridge to join Princeton and unfortunately, this fellowship went to another student, however Turing determined that the stipend from his fellowship at Cambridge would be sufficient funds to allow him to attend. That same year he received the Smiths Prize for research in mathematics and theoretical physics from Cambridge for his paper which aided him further to monetarily support himself at Princeton.

On September 23rd, 1936 Turing left for Princeton via ship, arriving in New York City on the 29th. On October 14th, he wrote to his mother about how his research was now asking the question "What is the most general kind of code of cipher possible?" To which he found that one of them was pretty impossible to decode without the key and though he expected that he could sell them to Her Majesty's Government this made him question the morality of his research if it could be put to use by the military.

After being denied a lecturer position in the spring of 1937 at Cambridge Turing decided to stay another year at Princeton where he was awarded a proctor fellowship and began studies for his Ph.D. thesis on the theory of numbers. In the Fall of 1937, Turing became distressed by the possibility of going to war with Germany, due to this he began theorizing about cryptanalysis specifically assuming that words would be translated to numbers on the binary scale from a code book he worried about these codes being decrypted if someone were to find the book, with this in mind he would multiply the number in the code by a secret number long enough that it would take one hundred Germans one hundred years to decode via routine search working eight hours a day on their desk calculators, this consideration is what brought the electric multiplier to life. With this new machine completed, Turing set off to build his third machine, this one specific to his thesis research intending to disprove Riemann's hypothesis by finding a point where the function had taken the value of zero at some point and Turing intended to search the next few thousand values to find it.

In March of 1938, his three-year fellowship was coming to an end and he had yet to receive word that Cambridge had extended it for him when he wrote home to ask a classmate to check on this and notify the college of his current research he added "I hope Hitler will have not invaded England before I come back". While he waited to find out if his fellowship had been extended he took his father's advice to look for employment in the US, though he was offered an assistant position at the Institute for Advanced Study once word came through that his fellowship had been extended he turned the position down. After submitting his thesis on May 17th, Turing received his Ph.D. from Princeton on June 22nd, 1938 in mathematical logic, and on July 18th embarked to return home with his electric multiplayer in toe wrapped in brown paper.

In the summer of 1938 Turing applied to work for The Government Code & Cypher School (GC&CS). It is unclear how Turing came in contact with them, though it is speculated that he may have been in contact since 1936 when he first theorized that his machine could have military applications. As of the late 1930s, there was an exponential influx of incoming codes from Italy and Japan divided over thirty staff members struggling to keep up, made worse in 1937 when it was established that Germany was using different versions of the same code across their military branches, the enigma system. While waiting for their response he gave lectures on mathematics at Cambridge, reportedly missing one class to go to another dedication to Christoper on the ninth anniversary of his death. In July 1939, the facility asked him to give his lecture on foundations of mathematics in spring of 1940 however on March 31st the British government committed to defend eastern Europe in alliance with France in response to Germany overtaking Czechoslovakia. Turing would not return to lecture in 1940 and would not return to mathematics, leaving all of the projects started in his two years back from the United States unfinished.

During this time Turing began working for the Government Code and Cypher School (GC&CS) at Bletchley Park, and after working extensively with Gordon Welchman. Considering his progress, October 2nd, 1939, Turing decided to suspend his fellowship at Cambridge for the duration of the war. In the fall, they presented sheets from the "Bombe" machine devised to decipher German Enigma Machine encrypted messages was brought to French cryptanalysts as a possible solution to the standstill experienced in decoding messages. By mid-1940, German Air Force signals were being read at Bletchley; previously they had not decoded any messages produced by the Enigma Machine since December. On September 4th, 1940 Turing began working in the codebreaking centre leading Hut 8, the section responsible for German naval cryptanalysis along with others such as Joan Clarke who came recommended by Welchman.

In their research Hut 8 developed a technique he called 'Banburismus', in order to decode the U-boat 'wolf-packs' messages. 'Ban' for the town of Banbury, England from which the sheets used were produced, in which a 'ban' of evidence made their hypothesis of the message description more likely to be true. After they secured captured Enigma material they found that the enigma machine only had two keys, one reserved for local correspondence and the other for communication over open water and began deciphering enemy supply randevu points, though this had become suspicious to Germany, the investigation they underwent showed that their cipher key had yet to be broken. From this the naval Enigma messages were able to be read from 1941.

After Turing's breakthrough he became engaged to Clarke. During this time period marriage was still viewed as a social duty as opposed to a union that one's sexual preference should be taken into account, this is a point Turing would bring up to Clark days after their engagement, specifically the fact that he had "homosexual tendencies" and did not expect their relationship to work out due to this, much to Turing's surprise Clark was unphased by this and Turing gave her a ring. Turing and Clarke never married, though they remained close friends for the duration of their lives despite this.

Turing traveled to the United States in December 1942, a year after they joined WWII, to advise US military intelligence in the use of Bombe machines and to share his knowledge of Enigma and in return he was made privy to the latest American progress on a top secret speech enciphering system. There were many encrypting projects that Turning may have been referring to including "Green Hornet" after the radio show The Green Hornet, due to the resemblance the sound of the buzzing to the show's theme song tune, to anyone trying to eavesdrop on the conversation, or the Code Talker project in which the Marines utilized Native Navajo speakers to create a code that would be used throughout the 2nd World War and later the Korean War. Turing returned to Bletchley in March of the following year, where he continued his work in cryptanalysis.

Following the fall of the North African port, Tobruk on June 21st, 1942 the authorities overseeing Bletchley insisted that those who were not a head of their section, such as Turing, participate in the home guard in their spare time. Though Turing was exempt he wanted to gain proficiency in rifle handling so he enrolled in the infantry of the home guard. Upon enrollment he filled out a form that included the question "Do you understand that by enrolling in the home guard, you place yourself liable to military law?" Turing chose to answer this question with "no" and once he was to his own standards proficient with a rifle, he stopped attending, when he was called to ask why he had stopped attending, he said he was not under military law and cited his form and he was unenrolled.

In 1943 Turing took a two month long excursion from January to March to the US mostly to work with Bell laboratory to assist in developing what is now known as SIGSALY, the first digital scrambled speech transmission system. He would pursue the idea of electronic enciphering with a communications machine with the code name *Delilah* after the biblical character who betrayed Samson in the Book of Judges; however its progress was stunted at various points. The first being the trouble Turing had finding an engineer to build the machine to match the mathematics he had worked out for, he had eventually found an engineer, Don Bailey, however this was not his only project and his higher ups pushed *Delilah* to the bottom of his priority list. An additional issue was that Bailey was appalled by Turing's non-chalantness regarding his homosexuality, though he was eventually able to chalk it up to another of many eccentricities, however with all of these setbacks, *Delilah* would not be completed in time for use during the war.

When asked what his plans were after the war he stated he planned to go back to his fellowship he had been on leave for since joining the war effort. Before he could do so, on May 27th, 1944 Kings opted to extend the fellowship from 18 months to 4 years and 6 months however he moved to the National Physical Laboratory (NPL) after the conclusion of the war in 1945 to produce his plans for the Automatic Computing Engine (ACE). Later in the year, Turing was awarded an Officer grade membership to the Order of the British Empire for his wartime work, subsequently the letters "OBE" were added to his office door at NPL however he did not appreciate the recognition, to the point that when his medal arrived was kept, hidden away, in Turing's tool box. On July 23rd, 1947, Turing's eccentricities became too much for the NPL to bear so he was sent back to Kings to "develop his theoretical ideas" for a year and on August 18th, construction began on the ACE to be completed by 1950. On September 30th, Turing would resume his fellowship at Kings as a sabbatical from NPL.

The culture of Cambridge had changed during the war, especially due to the fact that the student base was more so in their early 20's due to their service breaking up their education. This change of culture did not sway Turing from being open about his homosexuality, for example, when Robin Gandy, who was working towards a fellowship in theoretical physics, asked to borrow a book from Turning, when it was pulled from the shelf a newspaper clipping of page boys fell out and Turing came clean to him as a homosexual which was not an issue.

On May 28th, Turing accepted a position at Manchester as the Deputy Director of the Royal Society Computing Laboratory, despite starting too late to direct the building of the machine. Due to taking up this position, he resigned from the NPL despite there being two more years on his contract. On June 24th, 1949, at the inaugural conference of the Electronic Delay Storage Automatic Calculator (EDSAC), a quite similar machine to what Turing's laboratory was working on, that was released by University of Cambridge Mathematical Laboratory on May 6th, he gave a lecture titled "Checking a Large Routine" about the very real possibility of losing track of numbers in a long series as Turing had been writing for machines such as these for years prior, where as the team at Cambridge had only started that May, yet another instance of being ahead of his time.

July 9th through 12th of 1951, Turing attended the inaugural conference of the ACE machine, giving yet another lecture, this time about the Manchester machine code, though it was less well received, mostly described as "dry". This would be his last professional appearance regarding the coding or operation of computers because in December of 1951 Turing would meet 19-year-old Arnold Murray in Manchester.

They met on the street while Turing was shopping for Christmas presents, after catching his eye Murray was invited to lunch with Turing and later back to his house that evening however Murray chose not to show. The next week Turing spotted Murray on the street again, inviting him over to his house again, however this time to go right then as opposed to later, Murray accepted. By January, Murray was visiting on a regular basis and they began a physical relationship. As Murray was unemployed and Turing, being a minimalist, had more money than necessary and offered it to him of which Murray refused. Despite this, £10 turned up missing from Turing's wallet in the days following his visit on January 12th. Assuming Murray had stolen the money, Turing wrote to him saying he would like to end their acquaintance. Murray denied taking the money however admitted that he was in debt and asked for a loan of £3 to pay off the debt of which Turing gave as a gift. In a letter on the 18th, Murray asked for an additional £7 to pay off the remainder of his debt to which Turing asked where the money was owed to add legitimacy to Murray's story to which he complained about the lack of trust Turing had in him and was granted the money. On January 23rd, Murray would break into Turings' house with the assistance of an accomplice. Though he did not know for sure, he wrote to Murray again in an attempt to end their arrangement and for the £7 loan to be repaid.

Turing reported the burglary and during the investigation, Turing admitted to the police that he was in a relationship with Murray, where he explained that he was convinced that Parliament was just about "to legalize it" of which he was incorrect. Both he and Murray were arrested and prosecuted for "gross indecency" under Section 11 of the Criminal Law Amendment Act of 1885 however this came as a comfort to Turing as only 174 of the 746 men prosecuted under this charge faced jail time in 1951. Additionally, he was happy not to be charged with Buggery which was far more specific regarding different kinds of sexual acts.

The committal proceedings began on February 27st, 1952, after which Turing was released on a £50 bail, whereas Murray was held. Upon his release Turing wrote to his brother opening with "I suppose you know I'm a homosexual" then detailing what had happened so he could hear it from him as opposed to from the papers. In the letter Turing stated that he planned to plead "not guilty" to which his brother and later his legal counsel advised against.

The case, Regina v. Turing and Murray, was brought to trial on March 31st and at its conclusion Turing was sentenced to probation to go through 12 months of hormone treatment to reduce his sex drive resulting in chemical castration as opposed to imprisonment as his work was deemed too important for him to be imprisoned. Previously castration was not allowed in Great Britain however in the Criminal Justice act of 1948 stated that the community has a duty to provide treatment for the habitual sexual offender, of which gross indecency was lumped into.

In April 1953, his probation ended, however with his criminal record and the example made by two homosexual double agents for the Soviet Union, Guy Burgess and Donald Maclean, authorities from MI5 were convinced that Turing was a security threat as homosexuals were more liable to blackmail. Therefore he could not work for the Government Communications Headquarters (GCHQ), the British government's postwar code-breaking centre, or any research projects relating to the development of the computer.

On June 8th, 1954, Turing's housekeeper found him dead, the coroner determined that he had died the previous day at the age of 41, ruled as a suicide via cyanide poisoning speculated to be from the half eaten apple found by his body however the apple was never tested. Turing's remains were cremated on June 12th, 1954 and his ashes were scattered in the gardens of the crematorium where they had scattered his fathers ashes upon his passing on August 3rd, 1947. Turing's mother was on holiday in Italy at the time of his death, his mother, brother, and Lyn Newman, wife of his friend and coworker at the Royal Society Computing Laboratory, Max Newman, were in attendance.

In 2015 Alan Turings law was introduced implementing a pardon to men who were convicted "under historical legislation that outlawed homosexual acts" It is now informally contained in the Policing and Crime Act of 2017. In June of 2023, modeled after the posthumous pardon of Turing in 2013 the program pardoning those who were convicted of any offense related to homosexuality was extended to anyone regardless of gender identity, allowing female army veterans to have the service medals returned.

Al-Kassab, Fatima. "Women in England and Wales Can Now Be Pardoned for Old Convictions of Homosexuality." NPR, June 14, 2023.

Blamires, Cyprian P., Cyprian Blamires, and Paul Jackson. World Fascism: A Historical Encyclopedia. 1. Vol. 1. ABC-CLIO, 2006.

Darling, Harper-Hugo. "Evelyn Irons." Making Queer History, July 29, 2019.

Hodges, Andrew. Alan Turing: The Enigma: The Book That Inspired the Film The Imitation Game. London:

Vintage Publishing, 2014.

Lewis, Paul. "Evelyn Irons, War Reporter, Is Dead at 99." The New York Times, April 30, 2000.

"Four flowering plants that have been decidedly queered". Accessed November 24, 2023.

"Inside Story: A Woman of No Little Importance." The Telegraph, June 27, 2001.

CHAPTER SIX

SOVIET UNION

In the 15th and 16th centuries, sex between men was considered a sin in the Orthodox Church however patrons could use confession to pay penance for their sin and would rarely be disciplined otherwise. To embrace Westernization in 1716 Peter the Great introduced various reforms including banning homosexual activity specifically for soldiers in the Army and Navy. However, in 1832 Article 995 was added to the criminal code making sodomy (мужеложство) illegal and punishable by exile to Siberia for up to five years, in 1903, this was reduced to three months, and in 1917, all laws against sodomy were abolished in the wake of the Great October Socialist Revolution following the February Bourgeois Democratic Revolution earlier in the year that overthrew the Tsarist autocracy.

In 1926 the Soviet People's Commissariat of Internal Affairs prescribed regulations for intersex people (at the time referring to them as those "with the characteristics of hermaphroditism") who expressed interest in changing their name or have gender-affirming surgeries, intersex people were said to be treated as humanely as in any country in the world but only in parts of the Soviet Union, it was not as freely offered in Moscow or St. Petersburg. 36 people were identified, 27 from personal appeals and 4 identified by authorities during medical examinations for the military. Doctors trusted the intersex patient to make their own medical judgments, of the 36 individuals identified most had surgical operations, and some received hormone therapy.

On March 7th, 1934, during the Stalin era (1933-1953), Article 121 was added to their criminal code prohibiting male homosexuality again with the punishment of up to five years of prison labor. It was speculated that 800 to 1,000 were imprisoned each year. Later Soviet propaganda began depicting homosexuality as a sign of fascism which solidified the idea that this was used as a political tool to prove that Russia opposed the Nazi regime by cracking down on homosexuality as being immoral and comparing homosexuals to fascists like Nazis.

Though the Soviet Union had a more reasonable history with their homosexual population than many other countries explored here, they seem to be far more reserved; however we may explore the life of Guy Burgess, a homosexual, English State Security Committee (KGB) double agent for the Soviet Union who was utilized for his homosexuality to blackmail agents for information.

Guy Burgess

Guy Francis de Moncy Burgess was born on April 16th, 1911 in Devonport, England to father Commander Burgess of the Royal Navy and Evalyn Gillman and was older brother to Nigel Burgess. He was born to a family who had roots in keeping the British empire alive, not just in the four predominant nations but in the colonies, territories, and "protectorates" (areas in which England sought to protect the goods being output for them) as well. For example, there are claims that a Burgess ancestor paid off a Mohawk leader during the Revolutionary War in the United States to fight for the British, by 1805 William Robertson found himself on the east coast of what is now Canada after a shipwreck and would find himself fighting against the Americans during the War of 1812, in 1866 Burgess' grandfather, Colonel Burgess helped snuff out a rebellion within Arabia, fitting as his surname is derived from the same root word as Bourgeois.

In 1920 Burgess was sent to Lockers Park Preparatory School after beginning his schooling with a Governess at home and was to stay there until he was thirteen when he would transfer to the Royal Naval College Dartmouth where he was prized as "Excellent Officer Material" However after his fathers' death that same year Burgess began to rebel, the first instance of which he turned away from viewing the canings of classmates as was customary, later being accused of stealing. This was contested by his mother and the official reason for his departure from Dartmouth would be "eyesight problems" which would not allow him to be an officer however this is a point of skepticism as these problems were not noted at his intake and it was suggested by the college to sent him to Eton where he would eventually end up for the last three years of his pre-University education in 1927 where he joined his younger brother. Eton College is where Burgess claimed his homosexual experiences began, complete with a trip to "Queer Tangier " for his 18th birthday in 1929.

From 1923 to 1956 the city of Tangier was an international free zone that upheld its own laws as opposed to the laws of Morocco allowing it to become a haven for those interested in escaping the laws against homosexuality in their home counties. With this freedom, it saw the powerful minds of many writers including but not limited to Truman Capote, the author of *Breakfast at Tiffany's*, and Tenessee Williams, author of *A Streetcar Named Desire*. Later, Tangier would gain the title of being the world's first gay resort.

He won a scholarship to read modern history at Trinity College in Cambridge in 1930. During his time at Cambridge, it is reported that he made no attempt to conceal his homosexuality or apparent sadism, to the point where he became a matchmaker of sorts to his previous partners, however, it was noted that many of his previous partners were concerned about being blackmailed by Burgess as it was said that he never threw away a letter. Burgess would continue to sporadically see Michael "Micky" Burn, later WWII commando prisoner of war, poet, and journalist for *The Times* where he wrote *Guy Burgess: The Spy Who Loved Me and The Traitor I Almost Unmasked*.

At the time there was no communist student group at Trinity, so instead the communists recruited from the socialist clubs. Burgess joined the Labor Club (Cambridge University Socialist Society (CUSS) by 1934) with Kim Philby, Anthony Blunt, James Klugmann, and Donald Maclean. When Maclean and Klugmann joined the Communist Party of Great Britain in 1932: their main focus was to organize study groups and try to get Marxism accepted as a philosophy in the university curriculum.

Shortly after this Burgess would join the Apostles, the most exclusive club at Cambridge, with the recommendation of Blunt, which became a fantastic networking opportunity due to ample interactions with the great minds of his generation and those that came before that would intermittently attend these meetings as "Angels". He graduated in 1933 with his degree noting that he was unable to finish his work due to medical issues, however, he hung around the university attempting to write a thesis to become a fellow, however, this dream would not be actualized and he would disappear from the college records by spring of 1935.

In June 1934 Maclean graduated with honors and had intended to visit the Soviet Union to undertake voluntary work as a teacher or tractor driver, however, his mother encouraged him to join the British diplomatic service. Soon after Maclean was accepted into the Foreign Office he would come in contact with Arnold Deutsch, an Austrian physiologist at the University of Britain and an "illegal" which in terms of espionage would be someone acting as an intelligence agent without being an accredited diplomat who had asked Philby to make a list of recruits to serve as Soviet spies for the KGB, and the first person to be approached was Maclean. During his time in Britain, Deutsch would be credited with recruiting twenty agents and would be in contact with twenty-nine. Maclean suggested to Deutsch that he meet another one of his CUSS friends, Burgess. Deutsch rejected Burgess initially as a potential spy due to his drunkenness and desire to degrade himself, often leading to a slip of the tongue but Burgess began to suspect Maclean was working for the Soviets. He told Maclean: "Do you think that I believe for even one jot that you have stopped being a communist? You're simply up to something." When Maclean told Deutsch about the conversation, Deutsch had no choice but to sign him up as they believed it was more dangerous to the cause for him to be outside of the organization than inside and he was given the code name *Mädchen*.

The KGB would make good use of the contacts Burgess acquired over his time at Cambridge, especially with those whom he had met as part of the Apostles, specifically Dennis Proctor who at the time was attached to the office of Stanley Baldwin, who was effectively acting as Prime Minister during Ramsay

MacDonald poor health, of which Burgess suggested they recruit Proctor as well to which the leaders of his sect protested as they agreed he was too high profile. For other contacts such as Tom Willy, they were to use Burgess' sexuality to their advantage. After various interviews with the BBC Burgess, through lying about his mother being an invalid, was accepted into a training reserve to fill positions more quickly as they opened in July 1936 where he was among the first to be trained.

On January 1st, 1937 he was posted to the Talks department however due to his poor diction he was assigned to production as opposed to commentating making him responsible for selecting and interviewing potential speakers for current affairs and cultural programs for which he invited Blunt, writer and politician Harold Nicolson, Arabist St John Philby father of his CUSS counterpart, and British Prime Minister Winston Churchill who he knew socially. The talk with Churchill would not come to fruition despite an attempt on October 1st, 1938 to persuade him to reconsider his decision to withdraw from a talks series on Mediterranean countries.

During his acquisition of guests Burgess was able to cultivate a friendship with author David Footman, as asked of him by his controllers as they knew he was an MI6 officer. Upon his acquaintance Footman introduced Burgess to his superior at MI6, Valentine Vivian which resulted in Burgess carrying out several small assignments for MI6 on an unpaid freelance basis for the following 18 months.

Soon after he would be promoted to Talks Assistant and was put on a six month probation. Little of note happened in this time aside from the BBC having difficulties procuring a photo of Burgess for his file, rejecting two before accepting a photo that still bore little resemblance to him and in early 1937 Burgess had begun being treated for syphilis. After his probation he produced various programs including talks on art which featured fellow KGB agent Anthony Blunt who was asked back for a second program on forgotten art however from March 15th to April 27th, 1938 Burgess took time off of work following a letter from his doctor reached the BBC stating that he needed time away due to his nervous state and in a letter from McClean he may have suffered a nervous breakdown and insomnia and was being looked after by his mother in the south of France however evidence suggests he fled the country for a period following a dropped legal charge.

The department of propaganda in enemy countries under section D of MI6 was set up in March of 1938, with Burgess being made acquaintance in September and as this department recruited due to his radio experience, he was not vetted until September 1939 of which the response was "NRA" (Nothing Recorded Against). In December of 1938, Burgess resigned from the BBC, there are various conflicting accounts as to why he did this, especially because he had recently suggested that the BBC give a select few access to decoded transmissions made by government officials that would subsequently assist in decoding other communications from each nation. His departure became official on January 11th, 1939, the same month that the enemy publicity section was added as a branch of this department.

Burgess acted as Section D's representative on the Joint Broadcasting Committee (JBC), a broadcasting agency intending to work with the BBC to transmit anti-Hitler broadcasts to Germany while making it seem like these broadcasts were coming from Germany as opposed to the UK. After the outbreak of World War II in September, 1939, Burgess and Philby were moved to a training establishment in Brickendonbury Manor in Hertfordshire where he gave lectures on sabotage. In April of 1940, an additional branch was created under section D called DU of which Burgess was appointed assistant to the department head where his codename was DU1 however this was short lived as on July 22nd, section D and Special Operations Executive (SOE) merged, causing D to be put under new management and new scrutiny. On September 10th, Burgess was arrested for driving under the influence in a war office car, leading to him being under the lens. It is unclear when Burgess was let go, there are documents written by him dating into October however upon his release he rejoined the BBC in mid-January of 1941.

After Germany invaded the Soviet Union in June of 1941, the BBC had Burgess to select speakers who would depict Britain's new Soviet ally in a favorable light, in response Burgess arranged a broadcast by Soviet agent Ernst Henri who was masquerading as a journalist in 1942. In October of 1941 Burgess took charge of the political program *The Week in Westminster*, where he brought on people such as Labour MP Hector McNeil, a former journalist who served as a parliamentary private secretary in the Churchill war ministry.

In June of 1944, Burgess was offered a job in the news department of the Foreign Office explaining government policy to foreign editors and diplomatic correspondents. This gave Burgess an expansion of material of interest to Moscow, especially details about the upcoming Yalta Conference (Crimean Conference), held from February 4th to 11th, 1945, attended by Franklin D. Roosevelt, Winston Churchill, and Joseph Stalin and contingency plans for "Operation Unthinkable" a surprise assault to 'impose upon Russia the will of the United States and the British Empire'. By supplying this information Burgess was granted a £250 bonus.

In the 1945 general election, McNeil became Minister of State at the Foreign Office and in December 1946 secured Burgess as an additional private secretary, unaware of his communist alliances. Burgess made fast work of his new found clearance and in one six-month period transmitted 693 files, over 2,000 photographed pages to Moscow, for which he received an additional bonus of £200. Aside from a brief transfer in early 1948 for a position at the Foreign Office's newly created Information Research Department (IRD), to counteract Soviet propaganda, remained with McNeil until October 1948, when he was posted in China during the height of the Chinese Civil War. He returned to London for a new post in Washington starting in July of 1950 to replace Maclean who had been in the role from 1944 to 1948.

While in Washington he served on the inter-allied board responsible for the conduct of the Korean War, which gave him access to America's strategic war plans in addition to being chosen to act as escort to Anthony Eden, when the future prime minister visited Washington in November of 1950. In early 1951 after a series of offenses, including three speeding tickets in a day, he was ordered by the ambassador, Sir

Oliver Franks, to return to London on May 7th, 1951.

In 1951 the Foreign Office was being put under a tighter security check, looking for traces of Communist sympathies or of homosexuality and Guy Burgess and Donald Maclean disappeared, leaving London on May 25th. They had been reported in Rennes, France attempting to catch a train to Paris. From there they took a train to Bern, Switzerland where they secured false identities, including passports from the Soviet embassy. From there he arrived in Moscow by way of Zurich, Stockholm, and Prague.

On May 28th, Maclean's wife, Melinda would report him missing to the Foreign Office. After being held in Moscow Burgess and Maclean were sent to Kuybyshev where they were granted Soviet citizenship in October 1951 and Burgess took up the identity of "Jim Andreyevitch". Though the Soviets were also intolerant of homosexuality, eventually Burgess was allowed to retain a Russian lover, Tolya Chisekov. By early 1956 Burgess had moved back to Moscow, and found part-time work at the Foreign Literature Publishing House, promoting the translation of classic British novels into Russian. Maclean's wife and their children would join him in 1953 when he became a Soviet citizen and worked in the Foreign Ministry and the Institute of World Economic and International Relations.

Healey. Dan. Bolshevik sexual forensics: diagnosing disorder in the clinic and courtroom, 1917-1939. Northern Illinois University Press, 2009.

Healey, Dan. Homosexual Desire in Revolutionary Russia: The Regulation of Sexual and Gender Dissent.

Chicago, IL: University of Chicago Press, 2004.

.

Irvine, Amy. "Operation Unthinkable: Churchill's Postwar Contingency Plan." History Hit, April 21, 2023.

Morgan, Joe. "The Secret Gay History of Russia." Gay Star News, February 13, 2019.

Purvis, Stewart, and Jeff Hulbert. Guy Burgess: The Spy Who Knew Everyone. London: Biteback Publishing, 2016.

"Queer Tangier: What You Didn't Know about Morocco's Gay Phase." Out Adventures, December 15, 2022

CHAPTER SEVEN

CHINA

The earliest records of LGBTQ+ persons in China date from the Shang dynasty era (16th to 11th century BCE) with the term *luan feng* (鸞鳳) being coined to describe homosexuality where it was viewed with indifference. Though there were no records of lesbian relations in this time it can be assumed they would be treated with the openness that male homosexual relations were extended.

Homosexuality can be difficult to differentiate in Classical Chinese literature because pronouns were not distinguished as Chinese does not have grammatical gender; however several stories rose to popularity during the Zhou dynasty (1046 to 256 BCE). During the Han dynasty (202 BCE - 220 CE) the story *The Passion of the Cut Sleeve* (斷袖之癖) circulated about Emperor Ai of Han, one of the most famous Chinese emperors, and his male lover Dong Xian, after falling asleep for a nap on the same bed, Emperor Ai cut off Dong Xian's sleeve (in a piece of clothing they were sharing) rather than disturb him when he had to get out of bed. It was also during this period that one of the first mentions of female homosexuality surfaced. Additionally, during this period Ying Shao, a historian in the Eastern Han dynasty, made observations regarding several Imperial Palace women forming relationships referred to as *duishi* (對食) with its indirect translation interpreted to reciprocal cunnilingus.

The earliest law against homosexual prostitution in China dates from the Zhenghe era (1111 to 1118 BCE) of Emperor Zhao Ji in the Song dynasty (960 to 1279 BCE). These laws were to punish *nánchāng* (男娼), young males who act as prostitutes, with 100 strikes with bamboo canes and a cash fine, and *bu nan* (不男), male cross-dressing of which the punishment was not disclosed, however, it seems they were never enforced based on a lack of records. The first statute specifically prohibiting same-sex sexual intercourse was enacted in the Jiajing era (1522 to 1567 BCE) of Emperor Zhu Houcong in 1546. Despite this, homosexuality was still viewed as "luxurious" by the middle class. It was still commonly practiced, with the caveat that the men were still expected to marry women and produce heirs later on.

By 1655, the Qing dynasty (1644 to 1911 BCE) courts began to refer to the term *ji jian* (雞姦) for sodomy, and society began to emphasize strict obedience to the social order of heterosexuality. By 1740, voluntary homosexual intercourse between adults was made illegal, this was the first time homosexuality had been subject to legal proscription in China. The punishment included a month in prison and 100 strikes with bamboo canes, though, just as with the decrees in the Zhenghe era there were no records of the effectiveness of it.

By 1912, the 1911 Revolution toppled the Qing dynasty, and its explicit prohibition of *ji jian* was abolished by the succeeding states however at this point the heteronormative social structure had become mainstream through the Westernization efforts of the early Republic of China causing intolerance of gays and lesbians.

In this section we review the life of Nadine Hwang a Belgian and Chinese lesbian who, while living in France was outspoken regarding the tensions in northeast China during the French resistance, eventually leading her to the all-female concentration camp of Ravensbrück.

Nadine Hwang

Nadine Hwang (or Huong) was born March 3rd, 1902 in Madrid, Spain to a Belgian mother, Juliette Brouta-Gilliard, and a Chinese father, Lühe Hwang. Her father was transferred to Madrid as a diplomat due to his Spanish fluency and through her schooling Hwang spoke Castilian and French fluently, practiced Mandarin with other families of diplomats, and took English lessons. Due to the 1911 Revolution and the establishment of the Republic on January 1st, 1912, Hwang's father was transferred to Beijing in 1913 to the European Affairs Department of the Ministry of Foreign Affairs. Hwang continued her education in an international school run by French nuns then studied law at the American Hamilton College via distance learning from Beijing.

In a time in which the Chinese government was attempting to make changes to gender expression by banning footbinding in 1912, though the ban was not actively implemented, Hwang took it a step further as she liked to wear men's clothes, later identifying as a cross-dresser. This included appearing in traditional Aragonese costume in 1921 to dance the Aragonese Jota, a traditional courtship dance in northern Spain, with a female partner. This drew the attention of General Ye Ting who was forming an air force under Zhang Zongchang, the first Chinese warlord to accept women into his army in which Hwang would become a colonel.

She learned to drive a car and fly small planes at a very early age however in 1925 while on a trip to Paris financed by the Chinese Government with the intent of using her multilingualism and law background on a finance delegation, she started flying lessons at an airfield outside Paris, and returned to China as a trained pilot. In an interview with a journalist from Excelsior in 1928 Hwang states: "Everything fascinates me about these Western mechanics...I would love to sit on a locomotive and drive a train at full steam". Due to her education, the Chinese government continued to use her as a diplomat of sorts eventually sending her to Oregon, USA in 1927 to be press secretary for the Economic Information Service but by 1928 there was a coup against the Pan Fu government, and Nadine's diplomatic career ended as abruptly as it started.

In 1933, Le Petit Provençal, a newspaper based in Marseille, reported that Nadine arrived in France on a ship. In her time in France, she took part in women's rallies, where she was outspoken regarding the tensions in northeast China, and joined the literary salon of writer Natalie Clifford Barney, where she would become Barney's lover, driver, and secretary until 1940 when Barney would abandon Hwang moving to Italy to escape Nazi Germany with an artist girlfriend, while Hwang stayed in France, using her skills in the French resistance.

In 1944, shortly before the Allied liberation of much of France, she was deported to the all-female concentration camp of Ravensbrück for undisclosed reasons however as a homosexual and being active in the resistance movement there Hwang held various qualifications. Here she would meet the Belgian singer, Nelly Mousset-Vos, who was detained for spying.

After the war, and being removed from the Camp to Sweden during Operation White

Bus, she and Nelly moved to Venezuela. They began a new life posing as cousins while residing together. In the late 1960s, due to a stroke suffered by Hwang as a side effect of medication taken for a pre existing illness, they returned to Mousset-Vos' native Belgium where in 1972, Nadine passed away.

" History of Homosexuality." History of homosexuality. Accessed January 17, 2024.

Dehuai, Zou. "The Story of Nadine Hwang: The 'Chinese Joan of Arc.'" ThinkChina, November 18, 2022.

Harmsen, Peter. Shanghai 1937: Stalingrad on the Yangtze. Philadelphia: Casemate Publishers, 2015.

Hinsch, Bret. Passions of the cut sleeve: The male homosexual tradition in China. Berkeley, Calif: University of California Press, 1992.

Sommer, Matthew H. *Sex, Law, and society in late imperial china.* Stanford, CA: Stanford University Press, 2005.

CHAPTER EIGHT

UNITED STATES OF AMERICA

Though the US has roots in eugenics dating back to 1847, the writings of Robert Wilson Shufeldt in 1915, in a paper entitled *The Medico-Legal Consideration of Perverts and Inverts*, extended the practices of sterilization later defined "cruel and unusual punishment" from the "feebleminded" and people of color (of which he wrote about in his 1907 book *The Negro a Menace to American Civilization* and his 1915 book *America's Greatest Problem: the Negro*) to those who are plagued by "passive pederasty," "inversion," "perversion" and "homosexuality." Medical based research was being produced by Dr. J. Allen Gilbert, a physiology professor at the Medical School of the University of Oregon. Gilbert suggested a student of his, Alan Hart, go through with a hysterectomy in 1917, this would be the first time a hysterectomy would be sanctioned by a physician based on a patient's gender identity due using argument planted in eugenics that says that those with "abnormal inversions" be sterilized to their advantage. This would allow the Nazi party to validate their trends of eugenics by citing that the US was their ally in their movement in 1936, forcing the US to change their attitude towards eugenics starting with the 1942 *Skinner v. Oklahoma* case regarding Jack T. Skinner, a chicken thief, lessening the eugenics mandate against white-collar criminals, in 1981 Oregon performed the last legal forced sterilization.

Articles of War of the United States Article 93 wrote into law that "assault with intent to commit sodomy" would be illegal as of 1916, however on June 4th of 1920 Congress approved

a modification separating sodomy as a crime
itself.

In 1940 in Los Angeles Abraham Myerson
did a study testing for male hormones
(androgens) and female hormones (estrogens) in
the urine of 17 men tested for homosexuality
compared to samples from 31 heterosexual men
in an attempt to prove the chemical imbalance
that caused homosexuality. The results showed
that both sets of men had ratios of these
hormones that fluctuated by 13 points however
by averaging the results for each group
homosexual men were said to have a ratio of 60
androgens to 40 estrogens, leading to the theory
of chemical intervention being a possible solution
to curing homosexuality. To test this theory 11
homosexual men were dosed with additional
androgens, one via court order and three more
by parental authority. At the conclusion of the
test, three participants stated that they benefited
from it and five stated their homosexual drive
heightened. Another test had been done in a

different lab in 1940 with the opposite theory, that increased estrogen would cure homosexuality, instead they found it decreased libido towards either sex making it more effective than physical castration.

The implementation of a psychiatric screening for homosexuality during military induction beginning in 1941 when the US joined World War II following the attack on Pearl Harbor (1944 for Women's Army Corps) resulted in "Blue Discharges", a dishonorable discharge for those found "unfit for service". This would disqualify the service member from the GI bill and make it difficult to find work as you would have to show your discharge paperwork and the blue slip was well known.

To highlight how this mindset affected soldiers during World War II we will explore the lives of John Horne Burns, a gay man, who was a Harvard educated teacher at Loomis School in Windsor, Connecticut who was drafted in 1943 and Christine Jorgensen, a transgender woman, who was a photographer who attempted to enlist in 1944 but was denied, then drafted in 1945.

John Horne Burns

John Horne Burns was born October 7th, 1916 in Andover, Massachusetts as the first of seven children to a wealthy Irish lawyer. He was educated privately by the Sisters of Notre Dame at St. Augustine's School before moving on to a university prep school, Phillips Academy, where he pursued music. He attended Harvard, where he became fluent in French, German, and Italian graduating in 1937 with a degree in English and became a teacher at the Loomis School in Windsor, Connecticut. After five years at the school he would take a short recess due to his draft notice in 1942.

Though he was drafted into the US Army as a private, after attending the Adjutant General's School at Fort Washington, a school that was credited with turning out 300 trained officers every 60 days. he was Commissioned a second lieutenant. In 1943, he was sent overseas where he served in military intelligence in Northern Africa, specifically Casablanca, Morocco and Algiers, Algeria. In 1944 he was transferred to Naples, Italy where he would finish his service by censoring prisoner-of-war mail.

After his discharge in 1946 he returned to teaching at Loomis and finished writing his first of three published novels in April. Though he had written novels before, none had gone on to publishing. *The Gallery* was published in 1947 depicting fictional lives of various characters based in Allied-occupied North Africa and Naples in 1944. The title referred to the *Galleria Umberto I*, a shopping arcade in Naples that connects all of his characters because they have the same experience of passing by or through the arcade. Throughout the stories he explores resentment of the military, the struggle those feel when attempting to assert individuality, tension between officers and lower enlisted men and draftees, the psychological effects of dislocation, and the experience of homosexual military personnel.

Major newspapers such as the *New Yorker* and *Saturday Review*, and authors such as Ernest Hemingway praised the novel, and in a 1949 survey of the literature of World War II in *Military Affairs* credited Burns for the novel's "psychological study of rear echelon service personnel" in all areas except his depiction infantry combat which can be expected as he worked in intelligence as opposed to a frontline position. Though there are no lasting reviews that mention Burns' blunt homosexual longing within his pages he does take careful reference to men with "meaty thighs" leaning against a railing and soldiers in tight shorts in a bar.

Unfortunately, Burns' second and third novels were not received as warmly. The first of his two additional novels was *Lucifer with a Book*, a satirical representation of life at a boarding school published in 1949. As he was exceedingly disheartened by the critical reception Burns fled back to Italy in 1950, this time choosing Florence as opposed to Naples where he wrote his final novel *A Cry of Children,* which follows a composer and pianist which is speculated to have been modeled on his Harvard classmate Irving Fine. In 1952, On September 7th, 1952, *New York Times* critic James Kelly wrote "...nevertheless, reaffirms the author's status as one of America's gifted young writers. Perhaps his next one will bring both talent and subject-matter into sharper focus." Though he began work on a fourth novel, left unfinished as he died from a cerebral hemorrhage, thought to be caused by his excessive drinking on August 11, 1953. Later, Hemingway commented on Burns's brief life as a writer saying: "There was a fellow who wrote a fine book and then a stinking book about a prep school and then just blew himself up."

Christine Jorgensen

Christine Jorgensen was born George William Jorgensen, Jr. on May 30th, 1926 in the Bronx, New York City to parents George William Jorgensen, a carpenter and contractor, and Florence Davis Hansen, younger sibling of Dolly Jorgensen. In one of Jorgensen's early memories, she recalled questioning her identity to her mother asking: "Why didn't God make us alike?" to which her mother explained that the world needed both men and women and at the time there was no way of knowing the gender of the baby before it was born. While attending Christopher Columbus High School, Jorgensen developed an attraction to her male friends and upon reflection realized that she was not gay, instead, she was a woman trapped inside a man's body. This feeling turned to anguish after her sister's marriage, realizing that she could not have what her sister had with her marriage.

After Jorgensen graduated high school during World War II, in 1944, she tried to enlist in the Army, but she was denied because of her dainty size and weight, however, in 1945 she was drafted into the Army and stationed at Fort Dix, New Jersey. During Jorgensen's service, she kept mostly to herself and concealed her attraction to men; she stated that "I didn't go through basic training, I staggered through it." however she also stated: "I wanted to be accepted by the army for two reasons. Foremost was my great desire to belong, to be needed, and to join the stream of activities around me. Second, I wanted my parents to be proud of me."

After being honorably discharged in 1946, Jorgensen lacked direction; she attended Mohawk Valley Community College in Utica, New York, the Progressive School of Photography in New Haven, Connecticut, and the Manhattan Medical and Dental Assistant School in New York City. Along the way a book called *The Male Hormone* helped explain her problems, which led her to start taking estrogen in the form of ethinylestradiol, a common ingredient in birth control pills, before consulting with doctors about surgeons in Europe who had already performed sex reassignment surgery. Jorgensen was determined to be transformed into a woman, and in 1950, she traveled to Denmark to meet with endocrinologist Dr. Christian Hamburger at the Copenhagen *Serum Institut* who diagnosed Jorgensen as transsexual as opposed to homosexual going against what her previous physicians had labeled her as and he agreed to do the experimental procedure for free. For the next two years, Jorgensen underwent hormone treatment which increased the size of her mammary glands and assisted in regrowth of hair on her bald spot on her head. Additionally she underwent extensive psychiatric evaluations before being approved for a penectomy, the surgery to remove her male genitalia. Before she returned to the United States, she had one last alteration to make in order to complete her transformation, changing her name to Christine in honor of Dr. Christian Hamburger.

On December 1st, 1952, she made the front page of the *New York Daily News* under the headline "Ex-GI Becomes Blonde Beauty: Operations Transform Bronx Youth." the first article of many in the following months making Jorgensen realize that not only was this a dream coming true for her but "...this was an important step in the eyes of the world." showcasing not only advancements of technology and medical science but entertaining the idea of a shift in cultural ideology regarding the LGBTQ+ community until six months after the media released her story, reporters reached out to her surgeons as Jorgensen avoided questions relating to her anatomy by focusing on her war background and physical appearance and they were informed that Jorgensen removed her male genitalia but she did not have a vagina. Her former supporters began to claim that she could not be a woman without a woman's reproductive organs. She felt incomplete without a vagina until the day finally came, in May 1954, when

Jorgensen underwent a vaginoplasty performed
by Dr. Joseph Angelo and Dr. Harry Benjamin. In
1958 she would respond to the comments
belittling her womanhood stating; "Everyone is
both sexes in varying degrees. I am more of a
woman than a man... Of course I can never have
children but this does not mean that I cannot
have natural sexual intercourse – I am very
much in the position right now of a woman who
has a hysterectomy,"

She had several romantic relationships and
was engaged twice, first to labor union
statistician John Traub, then to typist Howard J.
Knox, but unfortunately, she was denied a
marriage license because her birth certificate
identified her as a male in 1959, losing Knox his
job when their engagement became known.

After her parents died, Jorgensen moved
to California in 1967, leaving behind the ranch
home built by her father in Massapequa to settle
at the Chateau Marmont in Los Angeles.
Jorgensen went on to be an entertainer and

performed in many nightclubs intending to be a Hollywood, however this dream would not come to fruition until 1970, Hollywood created a film based on Jorgensen's life called, *The Christine Jorgensen Story* after her autobiography written in 1967, *Christine Jorgensen: A Personal Autobiography* in which she highlighted thousands of letters, both positive and negative, but the majority of the letters were from others with the same problems asking for help and guidance. Jorgensen went on to use her story to lecture at colleges across the United States on gender identity during the 1970's and 1980's. On May 3rd, 1989, Jorgensen died from bladder and lung cancer and her ashes were scattered off Dana Point, California.

Berube, Allan. Coming out under fire: The history of gay men and women in World War Two. New York, NY:Penguin, 1991.

Bruccoli, Matthew J., and Ernest Hemingway. Conversations with Ernest Hemingway. Jackson: Univ. Press of Missisippi, 2001.

Burns, John Horne. The Gallery. New York: New York Review Books, 2014.

LaGrone, Sam, "Updated: History of U.S. Policy and Law on Gays in the Military." USNI News, March 27, 2018.

Margolick, David. "The Great (Gay) Novelist You've Never Heard Of." The New York Times, June 11, 2013.

McLaughlin, Matthew J. "Quantifying Sexual Constitution: Abraham Myerson's Endocrine Study of Male Homosexuality, 1938-1942." OUP Academic, September 23, 2021.

Poole, Rebecca. "From GI Joe to GI Jane: Christine Jorgensen's Story: The National WWII Museum: New Orleans." The National WWII Museum | New Orleans, June 29, 2020.

"Blue and 'Other Than Honorable' Discharges ." National Parks Service. Accessed July 5, 2023.

"Expressions as Diverse as the Landscape." National Parks Service. Accessed November 27, 2023.

CONCLUSION

Throughout this book, we are given the background of legal and cultural struggles of being an LGBTQ+ person residing in a country involved in either the Allied and Axis powers during the Second World War as well as accounts of individuals who had an effect or were affected by the war. From 1933 to 1945, according to the United States Holocaust Memorial Museum, an estimated 100,000 men were arrested for violating laws against homosexual acts, about half went to prison roughly 5,000 10 15,000 of these men were sent to concentration camps, and an estimated 60% did not survive.

In many cases, we see a regression in intolerance, such as the Soviet Union abolishing all laws against sodomy in 1917 in the wake of the Great October Socialist Revolution following the February Bourgeois Democratic Revolution. Earlier in the year that overthrew the Tsarist

autocracy and in 1926 the Soviet People's
Commissariat of Internal Affairs prescribed
regulations for intersex people but on March 7th,
1934, Article 121 was added to the criminal code
prohibiting male homosexuality again with the
punishment of up to five years of prison labor.

Now political wrongs are attempting to be
righted by the legalization of homosexual acts in
United Kingdom with the passing of the Sexual
Offences Act 1967 in England and Wales legalized
acts conditionally requiring that both men were
at least 21 years of age. This law was later
extended to Scotland in 1980 with the Criminal
Justice Act, and to Northern Ireland in 1982 with
the Homosexual Offenses Order as well as
implementing pardons in the United Kingdom
modeled after the posthumous pardon of Turing
in 2013 pardoning those who were convicted of
any offense related to homosexuality was
extended to anyone regardless of gender
identity, including female army veterans to have
the service medals returned, in 2014.

The United States reviewed discharges from 1945-1947 to upgrade the service members who had no proof against them committing homosexual acts to an honorable discharge. From 1945 to 1947 many of these discharges went under review and the service members who had no proof against them committing homosexual acts were upgraded to an honorable discharge giving them access to the GI bill. The blue discharge would be discontinued on July 1st, 1947 however due to other bills put into place homosexuals could not be in the military until the expiration of Don't Ask Don't Tell (DADT) which ran from 1993 to 2011.

On April 27, 1953, President Eisenhower signed Executive Order 10450, dubbed "The Lavender Scare" by historian David K. Johnson, to purge homosexual men and women from the federal government. The suffocating climate of fear and suspicion subsequently led to around 5,000 federal agency employees losing their jobs on the basis of their sexuality. Though terms such as "Lavender boy" would be associated with gay men back in the 1920s, the 1930s marked the start of a dark period when lavender was used to taunt Gay men in America for possessing a "dash of lavender" or a "streak of lavender", thanks in large part to Abraham Lincoln's biographer Carl Sandburg, who described the president's friendship with Joshua Speed who the president had admitted to sharing a bed with for four years, as containing a "streak of lavender, and spots soft as May violets."

In Italy, a plaque honoring 53 men who were exiled for their homosexuality was dedicated on June 8th, 2014, with the addition of a bell hanging above it rung at 8:00pm to commemorate when they would be locked in their barracks until the following morning, on October 18th of the same year in France, officials in Paris had a memorial plaque installed at the site of the arrest of the last people to be put to death for sodomy, Jean Diot and Bruno Lenoir.

Today it is legal to marry a same-sex partner in 34 countries including France in 2013, the United Kingdom in 2014, the United States in 2015, and Germany in 2017, and civil unions for same-sex partners are legal in Italy as of 2016. On September 10th, 1980, The Marriage Law of the People's Republic of China (中华人民共和国婚姻法) defined marriage as a union between a man and a woman. On January 5th, 2016, a court in the southern Hunan Province, agreed to hear the first case of gay marriage rights in mainland China, a lawsuit filed by 26-year-old Sun Wenlin, who in June 2015 was refused permission to marry his 36-year-old partner, Hu Mingliang in December, however, on April 13th, 2016 the Changsha court ruled against Sun. Despite this, on May 17th, 2016, Sun and Hu were married in a private ceremony in Changsha and expressed their intention to organize another 99 same-sex weddings across the country in order to normalize same-sex marriage in China. In October 2017, the National People's Congress amended Chinese law so that "all adults of full capacity are given the liberty of appointing their own guardians by mutual agreement." The system, variously called "legal guardianship" or "guardianship agreement", permits same-sex partners to make important decisions about medical and personal care, death and funeral, property management, and maintenance of rights and interests, in which their legal relationship can also include wealth and inheritance, or pension.

Though wrongs are attempted to be righted it is important to hear the stories that are so frequently written out of history. Were Alan Turings' achievements any less due to his sexuality? But in the same vein, Ernst Röhm was not more in the right than any other Nazi just because he was *gleichgeschlechtlich*. People should not be written into or out of history due to their sexuality or gender identity, the presence of these people in history is paramount to the acceptance of the LGBTQ+ community to show that this is not a new ideology, it has been part of the human story since the beginning and without learning about some of these people we are missing key aspects of trying times in history.

EPILOGUE

This book is not intended to be a comprehensive list of stories of all LGBTQ+ who were affected by or had an effect on World War II, each name was carefully selected however throughout this research there were instances in which someone had historical significance to the LGBTQ+ however information regarding their whereabouts during World War II have been lost over the years. That is the intention of this book, to make these stories more attainable before they are lost to history, one of which is Alan L. Hart, whose whereabouts during World War II have been speculated due to the social and political context of the United States during this time so I did not feel that I had enough information about him during the time period to keep him in the United States section however I

did not want his story to be lost further than it
had been so he will live in this epilogue.

Alan Hart

Alan Hart was born Alberta Lucille Hart,
but went by Lucille, on October 4th, 1890 in Halls
Summit, Kansas to Albert and Edna Hart.
Unfortunately, Albert would pass away two years
after Hart's birth and Edna would move them to
Albany, Oregan shortly after. Once Hart was old
enough to understand his father's death he
would comfort his mother with the sentiment
that he would grow up to become a man and
take care of her.

He attended Albany High School where he
fantasized about becoming his female high
school teacher's husband and graduated second
in his class in 1908. Upon graduating he enrolled
in Albany College before transferring to Stanford
University in 1910 to join the premedical
program.

In 1913 Hart enrolled in the Medical School of the University of Oregon where he found himself confiding in Dr. J. Allen Gilbert, a physiology professor at the University, about the dysphoria he was feeling about his female gender and female-oriented sexuality. Initially, he was confiding in Gilbert to convert himself into a conventional woman, they tried therapy and hypnosis before Hart was repulsed by the realization that if the conversion worked he would no longer feel like a man.

He graduated in 1917 and was awarded the Saylor medal for being the top scholar in each of the schools' departments as he was head of his class and was labeled as the first woman to win this medal as he was presently living as a woman at that time. In 1918 a fellow student wrote about Hart in the Spokane *Spokesman-Review*, a newspaper servicing the inland Northwest states. In their article, they wrote: "She had the distinction of being the only woman in the class.... She dressed often in a very mannish style, wearing particularly masculine hats and shoes and frequently tight skirts. She walked with a noticeable mannish stride."

Gilbert suggested Hart go through with a hysterectomy in 1917 and Hart would undergo the operation in the winter between 1917 and 1918 which was followed by a legal name change to Alan Hart. In 1920, Gilbert would write Hart in as "H" in an article about the treatment of homosexuality which would not be tied back to him until 1976.

In November, he was hired as an intern at San Francisco Hospital as a man. He roomed with a fellow male intern and kept a picture of Inez Stark on his wall claiming she was his wife, though they were not officially married however they were romantically involved. Unfortunately, Hart was still recognizable to former classmates from Stanford and as one recognized him when applying for a job they mentioned it to hospital staff. On February 5th, 1918, the *San Francisco*

Examiner printed an article with the headline "Girl Poses as Male Doctor in Hospital" and the *Oregon Daily Journal* "Intern Unmasked as Girl Graduate of Oregon School" followed by the *Austin American* the next day with "Woman Poses as Man Interne in Hospital at Frisco".

He would flee San Francisco with Inez to Gardiner, Oregon where he married Inez in the Congressional church that February and attempted to continue practicing this time at his own medical practice. On March 26th a response article came out from an interview Hart did with the *Albany Daily Democrat* saying "For years I had been unhappy. With all the inclinations and desires of the boy, I had to restrain myself to the more conventional ways of the other sex. I have been happier since I made this change than I ever have in my life, and I will continue this way as long as I live... I came home to show my friends that I am ashamed of nothing." Unfortunately, this series of events would repeat later in 1918 as he tried to continue practicing in

Gardiner, Oregon where he was outed again and moved again. By September of 1923, this became too much for Inez and she left, eventually asking for a divorce and cease of contact in 1925 which allowed Hart to marry his second wife Edna Ruddick that same year. In 1928 Hart graduated from the University of Pennsylvania with a master's degree in radiology and with this training, his research would be paramount to those with tuberculosis as many patients were asymptomatic and were able to be treated before complications arose.

During World War II, Hart worked as a medical adviser at the Army Recruiting and Induction headquarters in Seattle. Though it was unclear what he was tasked with at the Recruiting headquarters, due to his background it is unlikely that he was part of the implementation of a psychiatric screening for homosexuality due to his lack of specialization in psychiatrist, more likely he would fill gaps of specialists needed in order to complete these screenings, subjecting himself to being found out as being born female while married to a woman. However, after WW2, synthetic testosterone became available in the US as it was invented in 1935 in Amsterdam, allowing Hart to grow a beard and develop a deeper voice, which made him more confident in public interactions. In 1948 Hart graduated with a second master's degree from Yale University in public health.

On July 1st, 1962 he passed away from heart disease in West Hartford, Connecticut.

DeLuca, Leo. "Trailblazing Transgender Doctor Saved Countless Lives." Scientific American, August 26, 2021.

Gilbert, J. Allen. "Homo-Sexuality and Its Treatment." Journal of Nervous and Mental Disease, 1920.

Head, Tom. "100 Years of Forced Sterilizations in the U.S." ThoughtCo, August 9, 2021